THE PERFECT INTERVIEW

Your Key to Acing Job Interviews!

Dan Quillen

Author of *Get a Job! How I Found a Job When Jobs are Hard to Find –
And So Can You!* and *The Perfect Resume*

Cold Spring Press

Get a Job! series

The Perfect Interview is the third in the **Get a Job! series** of books written by Dan Quillen. Once again, Quillen calls on his expertise as an HR professional (and as one who lost and found a job in the toughest economic environment since the Great Depression) to help his readers understand the New Economy, and how to find work when many cannot.

CITATIONS

Billie Jean King quote: *www.brainyquote.com/quotes/quotes/b/billiejean121917.html*

(First) Mark Twain quote: *www.twainquotes.com/Statistics.html*

Babe Ruth quote: *www.baberuth.com/quotes*

Benjamin Franklin quote: *www.brainyquote.com/quotes/quotes/b/benjaminfr138217.html*

Wayne Gretzky quote: *www.brainyquote.com/quotes/quotes/w/waynegretz378694.html*

Paul "Bear" Bryant quote: *www.coachlikeapro.com/coach-paul-bear-bryant.html*

Mike Singletary quote: *www.brainyquote.com/quotes/quotes/m/mikesingle127505.html*

Pelé quote: *www.beliefnet.com/Quotes/Sports.../The-More-Difficult-the-Victory.aspx*

Anna Wintour quote: *www.marieclaire.co.uk › Features*

Tom Landry quote: *www.brainyquote.com/quotes/quotes/t/tomlandry154664.html*

Ted Williams quote: *www.beliefnet.com/Quotes/Sports-Inspiration/T/Ted.../Keep-Going.aspx*

Laird Hamilton quote: *lockerdome.com/6170049387962945/4602939445625362*

(Second) Mark Twain quote: *www.brainyquote.com/quotes/quotes/m/marktwain103892.html*

PRAISE FOR DAN'S JOB-SEARCH BOOKS!

"I was out of work for almost 2 years, and was just not getting many responses from the resumes I was sending out. I picked up a copy of Dan's book and began following his counsel in a number of areas, especially related to resumes and interviewing. Within 3 weeks, I had 4 interviews and received two job offers. I am now happily employed with a great job and feel like following Dan's counsel is the primary reason I was able to get these job offers and land my job." – *Jeremy Savage*

"Dan Quillen knows what he is talking about in this book. I took his advice and had a job within 3 weeks of being laid off. Buy it today and it will set you on a direct course to success!" – *Lynette W. Fox*

"Mr. Quillen's book is an easy read with a great deal of helpful information. Having been a hiring manager and HR director, as well as having been laid off himself during the recent recession, Mr. Quillen has a particular expertise that others may not. This book is also written with a focus on how techniques in job searching have changed in recent years, due to technology and the economy. I highly recommend this book to those that are either newly unemployed or wishing to make a change." – *Debra S. Heglin*

"If you want to spend your money wisely on creating a résumé that will result in interviews and therefore job offers, this book will take you further and more expeditiously than most so-called experts. He gives clear, simple, succinct direction in *Get a Job!* to create a résumé that will get the interview to get the job! Don't skip any chapters!" – *Ginny Ford, Ford Personnel, Inc.*

"I have been recommending *The Perfect Resume* to all my candidates. I love the content and the order of things that are presented in Dan's book." – *Sally S. Cohen, President, The Arundel Group*

COLD SPRING PRESS
www.get-a-great-job.com

Copyright © 2014 by W. Daniel Quillen
ISBN 13: 978-1-59360-207-9
Library of Congress Control Number: 2014946885

ABOUT THE AUTHOR

Dan Quillen is the author of *Get a Job! – How I Found a Job When Jobs are Hard to Find, And So Can You!* and *The Perfect Resume*. He has been a professional in Human Resources for more than twenty years. For a decade, he was the Director of Human Resources for one of the largest law firms in the western United States. Currently he is the Director of Internal Services (managing Human Resources, Purchasing, Risk and Fleet) for the City of Aurora, the third largest city in Colorado.

For years, Dan has been an active mentor for those who are out of work, freely sharing his expertise in résumé review and creation, interviewing and job searching. A few years ago Dan was laid off and had the opportunity to try the techniques he has been teaching others for years. In *Get a Job!*, Dan shares the knowledge and techniques that allowed him to find a job in a short period of time during the worst economic downturn our country has had since the Great Depression.

When not doing HR, Dan is a professional writer specializing in travel, technical, genealogy, and how-to subjects. He has written and published fourteen books on various topics. Dan makes his home in Centennial, Colorado. If you'd like to contact Dan about anything in this book, his e-mail address is: wdanielquillen@ gmail.com, and he welcomes your comments and questions.

Table of Contents

THE PERFECT INTERVIEW

Your Key to Acing Job Interviews!

Introduction

Don't be upset by the results you didn't get, with the work you didn't do.
— Internet Wisdom

Welcome to *The Perfect Interview*, and thank you for purchasing this book (or at least checking it out from your local library!). This job-interview manual is the third in a series of books designed to help you find work in this most difficult economy — this **New Economy**. It is a follow-on book to *Get a Job!*, the first in this series and a companion to *The Perfect Resume*, the second book in the series.

I wrote *Get a Job!* when I was laid off in the midst of the Great Recession. As an HR professional for the past two-plus decades, I knew what it took to get a job. Or so I thought. I learned very quickly that the job-search market had changed immensely since the last time I had actively looked for work. In previous years, a squeaky-clean resume, dressing sharply and establishing a rapport with hiring managers was enough to ensure you a new job.

That is no longer the case. Don't get me wrong — those items are still important, but they no longer set you apart from the masses. Everyone has a competent resume, dresses well and (generally) speaks well. I learned I had to be better — have a better resume, pay careful attention to my dress and have a plan and a purpose to my interview beyond just answering questions in a manner that didn't automatically eliminate me from competition.

Why did I write this book? And for that matter, why did I write all these books about finding work in this New Economy? I did so for several reasons. First, as an

HR professional, I am constantly amazed at the number of people who don't have a clue about successfully seeking work in the current economic environment. Second, I like to help people. Third, one of my passions is writing, and these books were a way to combine all those elements. Mostly, though, I just want to help people find work. My heart goes out to the legions upon legions of people who are out of work today, or who are severely under-employed. Often, they (you) find themselves in this condition through no fault of their own. And this New Economy is the toughest economy for job searchers our nation has known since the Great Depression.

I'm also mad. It angers me to see our government tell people that unemployment is at a moderate 6-point-something percent. If you are reading this book, you know that isn't the truth. If you look around yourself at your friends, neighbors and family members, you know the number is much higher. We'll talk a little more about that in the next chapter.

About now, you may be asking yourself several questions. Let's see if I can answer those questions, along with a few you haven't yet thought of:

What qualifies this guy to write this book?

I have been a Human Resource professional for over two decades, and for longer than that, I have been a hiring manager. I know what hiring managers and HR departments look for when they interview applicants for a position. And – perhaps more important – I know what works and what does not work for applicants when it comes to interviews.

Does this guy know anything about finding work in the New Economy?

Yes – several years ago, at the height of the Recession, I found myself suddenly out of work. I walked the path you are walking, and I know what it takes to work to get an interview, and then to sit across from a recruiter / HR professional / hiring manager in an interview. I have done it, and I have done it in the New Economy. I know that you can have the best resume possible, but if you aren't comfortable interviewing, you'll not close the deal and get the job.

Why is this guy writing this book?

I have to be honest (I always am!) – it appalls me to see how little so many candidates know about searching for jobs. It is almost stunning to see the naïveté of many job searchers on an almost daily basis. Through the pages of this book (as well as the pages of the other books in this series) I will give job seekers better odds in finding work.

My hope is that this book will help you learn a few things that will help you get interviews and succeed when you are able to interview.

I am interested to hear how things are going in your job search. When you have a chance, please e-mail me at wdanielquillen@gmail.com and let me know how it is going, your successes and even some of your questions.

Introduction checklist

_____ The New Economy has changed the way I have to look for work!

_____ Dressing well and having a squeaky-clean resume isn't enough anymore.

_____ The New Economy is the toughest economy for job searchers our nation has seen since the Great Depression.

_____ This guy seems to have the pedigree / background to know what he's talking about!

_____ Pick up a copy of *The Perfect Resume*.

_____ Pick up a copy of *Get a Job!*

Listen to what this guy says: he's walked in my shoes!

Overview

Champions keep playing until they get it right. – Billie Jean King

Thank you for your interest in *The Perfect Interview*! In this book, we'll spend a little time together, discussing information you should know about all the pertinent elements of interviews – preparation for, likely questions, dangers to be aware of, the interview itself and follow up. I have interviewed many upon many individuals through the years, and have some definite opinions on what works – and what does not! So if you'll read on, you'll learn more about how to get interviews and how to succeed in them. (**Note**: success = new job.)

This is a tough economy – the toughest in over eight decades, since the Great Depression. So many Americans are out of work, and most jobs these days have hundreds of applicants. You need to find a way to earn an interview, and then you need to shine in the interview you've worked so hard to get.

Following is what I will share with you in *The Perfect Interview*:

In **Chapter 1**, *Introduction*, we talked about the toxic New Economy, and I outlined my credentials that allow me to write this book – not only my two-plus decades of HR work, but the fact that I lost my job during this New Economy, and was able to find a new job within a very short time.

OVERVIEW

In **Chapter 2**, *Overview*, I am providing you with a quick summary of each of the chapters you'll read in this book.

In **Chapter 3**, *The Current Economic Environment*, we'll explore the difficulties of the current economic environment – the New Economy. You'll learn about the difference between the number the Federal government reports as the unemployment rate, and the real unemployment rate. I doubt you'll be surprised when you learn what the real unemployment rate is, and how it should be calculated. (Hint – if you have been out of work for longer than four weeks, the official government numbers do not include you as unemployed.)

In **Chapter 4**, *How to Get That Interview*, we'll address the things you'll need to be doing to secure the interview that may end your unemployment. You'll learn some of the key elements that will put you at the head of the pack of candidates when it comes to trying to land an interview. We'll talk about detailing, tailoring, networking, scheduling, researching and preparing.

In **Chapter 5**, *Kinds of Interviews*, we'll discuss the kinds of interviews you are likely to run into during your job search. Learn why telephone interviews are as important as face-to-face interviews with hiring managers. We'll talk about interviews with HR departments and recruiters, and how to succeed in those interviews. And – at the end of the day, you'll have to interview with the hiring manager, the decision maker, and you must succeed in that interview.

In **Chapter 6**, *Kinds of Questions*, I'll introduce you to the kinds of questions you are likely to experience once you get to an interview. What's the difference between a behavioral question and an informational question? How do you best answer those questions? What about "What if?" questions? How do you handle those? We discuss these and other kinds of questions you are likely to encounter, and I share my thoughts on what it takes to be successful in answering those questions.

In **Chapter 7**, *Preparing for Your Perfect Interview*, I'll share some of the tactics, practices and tips that have worked for me and for many whom I have mentored through the years in interview preparation. Follow these steps and you will likely be as prepared as you can possibly be for your interview. Ignore this chapter and the information there, and you may wish you hadn't! During the chapter I share some specific things to do that will help you feel confident as you approach your interview – don't skip this chapter! You'll note that this is one of the longest chapters in the book…that is because the principles I address in there are some of the most important of the book.

In **Chapter 8**, *Your Perfect Interview*, celebrates the fact that you've landed the perfect interview for the perfect job – and then gives you pointers on how to succeed during the interview. We'll discuss elements like the 20-20-20 rule, dressing for success, timeliness, business etiquette, dangerous questions to prepare for, and follow-up.

In **Chapter 9**, *Dressing for the Perfect Interview*, we'll continue the discussion on the need to dress appropriately for your interview in order to make the best impression. You may be surprised at some of the fashion tips you'll find there.

In **Chapter 10**, *I am Getting Interviews, But No Job*, we'll investigate what might be happening in your interview that is causing you to miss out on achievement of your goal – becoming employed. Some of the things we discuss may be surprising to you.

In **Chapter 11**, *I am Just Not Getting Any Interviews*, we'll focus on the companion problem explored in the previous chapter.

Chapter 12, *How to Ruin an Interview*, is one of my favorite chapters in this book! I'll share career-stunting actions you can do to sink an interview. Some of them will cause your rapid dismissal as a candidate. Most, if not all these actions have been demonstrated to perfection in interviews I have had with candidates through the years.

OVERVIEW

In **Chapter 13**, *Considerations for Recent College Graduates*, we'll address topics that are particularly relevant to those who are just graduating from college. While most of these will be young people, that may not be the case all the time – many mid-career older workers are returning to college to obtain that degree they started decades before.

In **Chapter 14**, *Stay Positive!*, we'll discuss ways to stay positive during your job search, ways to keep your energy up and focused. It's important for you in so many ways. We'll discuss the importance of that positive attitude and how your attitude – positive or negative -- may carry over in your resume, cover letter and interview.

At the end of each chapter, I have provided you with a checklist, sort of a summary of what was covered in the chapter, and a reminder of things you should – and shouldn't! – do to be successful in your job hunt.

So let's go – strap on your job search seatbelt, and let's figure out how you can make this unemployment chapter in your life as short as possible!

Success in an interview = a new job!

Overview checklist

_____ I should scan this chapter and select the chapters that are most relevant to my job search.

_____ Read those chapters I have singled out. Learn from them.

_____ But don't just cherry-pick! If I ignore certain chapters (*Preparing for Your Perfect Interview*, or *How to Ruin an Interview*, for example), I may get an interview and bomb because I didn't learn and heed the messages in this unread chapters.

_____ While I don't need to read the book sequentially, each chapter has been developed from years of working in this job search business – on both sides of the interview desk – and the points and topics covered are important for me to be successful.

_____ Read this book, put into practice the things that are contained therein, and get a job!

The Current Economic Environment

There are three kinds of lies: lies, damned lies, and statistics.
– Mark Twain and others

Of the above quote, Wikipedia says:

> Lies, damned lies, and statistics is a phrase describing the **persuasive power** of numbers, particularly the use of statistics to **bolster weak arguments**. It is also sometimes colloquially used to doubt statistics used to prove an opponent's point. (Bolding added)

It is an apt description of the statistics provided monthly by the government trying to convince us that the economy is improving / has improved.

As stated in Chapter 1, this New Economy is the toughest economy for job searchers our nation has known since the Great Depression. It is a time when every job has many applicants, and job hunters have to know how to get their resume into the hands of hiring managers, and then to have that resume pique their interest – enough to have them pick up the phone and call for an interview.

This is a difficult economic environment in which to find yourself seeking employment – as of this writing, over 20,000,000 Americans are out of work or severely under-employed – a staggering number. That's about one in seven Americans who are or wish to be in the workforce who is not.

For whatever reason, the Federal government continues to publish unemployment numbers they know are simply not true – perhaps they mean them as a goal or aspiration, but they certainly do not represent the true unemployment rate in the United States. At the time of this writing, the number they are publishing is 6.1%. This number is the number of those individuals the government categorizes as unemployed because they are considered to be actively looking for work. They do not include, however, those who have been out of work for longer than four weeks... that's right – four weeks. Thirty days. One hundred-sixty work hours. They assume individuals who have been out of work longer than four weeks have decided they don't want to work, and therefore should not be considered as unemployed. The government categorizes them as "discouraged workers eliminated." So – I guess the good news is that if you have been out of work for longer than four weeks, you are no longer considered unemployed…congratulations!

Neither does the official unemployment number include those who have taken part-time jobs – even with cuts in salary of tens of thousands of dollars – to try and make ends meet while they continue to look for full-time employment.

The government tracks another employment number they do not talk much about (but which is available if you know where to look). That number does include those who have been out of work for longer than four weeks, but less than one year.

While the economy seems to be perking up a little at the time of this writing (mid-2014), the United States Bureau of Labor Statistics' own numbers tell us that in the last year or so, seven out of eight jobs that were created were part-time jobs. The reason? There are many, I am sure, but one reason is that employers are cautious about hiring full-time workers while the economy is so fragile.

Another reason so many part-time jobs are being created is the **Affordable Care Act** (commonly referred to as **Obamacare**). Obamacare dictates to employers that they must provide health insurance to any workers who work over 30 hours a week on a regular basis. Employers therefore hire workers for 20 to 25 hours. Where they used to hire one employee for a 40-hour-a-week job, now many of employers hire two 20-hour workers so they don't have to pay for health-care benefits.

Back to the unemployment rate. The Bureau of Labor Statistics also has another number – and that number includes **those who have accepted part-time jobs but are still searching for full-time employment**. It also includes those who have been unemployed for up to a year. That number, called **U6** – is around 13% at the time of this writing. And that number feels much closer to me, given the number of family, friends and acquaintances I have that are currently out of work.

Notwithstanding the U6 number, many respected economists think the unemployment rate is as high as 25% – approaching the percentages seen in the Great Depression. Personally, I think the true number is someplace between the U6 number and 25%. (Note – the 25% number includes the items the U6 number includes, but also includes those who have been unemployed for longer than one year.)

Suffice it to say – the economy isn't getting better any time soon, for many reasons. But let's not focus on that – let's focus on ways to help you beat this economy and land a job.

Another symptom of the New Economy, as you might surmise, is that there are many candidates for each job opening. I work for the third-largest city in Colorado. Every Monday morning, we have New Employee Orientation for those candidates who have been successful in earning jobs at the city. Each Monday morning, I take a few moments and greet those new employees and welcome them to the city. As part of my time with them, I share how many people they beat to get their job. During 2013, our city averaged 157 applicants per job opening…and that doesn't include the applicants for our Police or Fire openings – those routinely attract between 2,500 and 3,000 applicants!

And so it is with the New Economy across the nation. While there are many open jobs, because of the high (higher than 6-point-something percent!) unemployment rate, there are also many applicants per job. You must understand how to turn the odds in your favor by learning how to get interviews, and then how to shine during those interviews. And that's what we'll be talking about in the upcoming chapters!

> **Be wary of the employment numbers you hear reported in the media.**

Overview checklist

_____ There are three kinds of lies: lies, damned lies, and statistics. The government is adept at all three kinds!

_____ Many Americans are out of work – I am in good company!

_____ US unemployment numbers as reported are far from accurate.

_____ The U6 unemployment number may be a more accurate gauge of US unemployment, although many economists feel even that number is still too conservative…but it's closer.

_____ The New Economy features many applicants for each open job.

How to Get That Interview

Never let the fear of striking out get in your way.
– Babe Ruth

Face it – without an interview (or numerous interviews) you are not going to get a job. You can research companies, talk to people (network), revise your resume dozens of times, etc., but until you land an interview, you are not going to end your unemployment.

In this chapter, we'll discuss important aspects of your job search that if attended to, will help you get interviews. Those areas are:

- Your resume

- Networking

- Set a schedule

- Set goals

YOUR RESUME

First things first – you must have a resume. You must have a good resume. You must have a resume that is appealing to the hiring manager whose eye (and interest) you are hoping to catch. And – *this is very important* – do not try to use the same resume for all jobs to which you apply – it simply will not work. To be successful, you will need to tailor your resume to the jobs for which you apply.

Let's discuss each of those items one at a time:

A good resume. What constitutes a good resume? A good resume is one that yields critical information about you rapidly and in a manner that is easy for the reviewer to locate. You want your critical skills, expertise and capabilities to leap off the page at the hiring manager, HR department or recruiter. It must be laid out well, in a format that makes sense and that accentuates the positive aspects of your experience and candidacy. I spend a great deal of time in my book *The Perfect Resume* discussing some of these points – check it out.

An appealing resume. An appealing resume is one that is easy on the eyes, and invites exploration. It's not cramped looking, not so filled with prose that it looks like a term paper. You should be able to lay your resume on the table, and without reviewing the content, it must be visually appealing. You should have plenty of white space: ample margins at the top, bottom and sides. It should make judicious use of formatting – bolding, italicizing, indenting, etc. Don't go overboard, but you want your resume to stand out among your competitors' resumes.

An appealing resume just plain looks good. It feels professional.

A tailored resume. Make no mistake about it: you must tailor your resume for each job to which you apply. If you do not, I can almost guarantee you that your search will take longer than if you tailor your resume for each job.

When I lost my job during the Recession, I learned very quickly that it was necessary to revise my resume to address each and every job for which I was applying. Over my four months of unemployment, I applied for 130 jobs. I probably used 120 different resumes to apply to those jobs. Was I successful doing this? Yes, I would say so. While my peers – other job hunters whom I met through networking groups – were getting one interview for every twenty or twenty-five resumes they submitted – about a 4% or 5% hit rate. At the same time, in the same nasty job-search environment, I was enjoying a nearly one-in-four hit rate on my resume submissions – for the 130 jobs for which I applied, I received 31 interviews – a 23.8% rate of success.

Why?

Because I worked very hard to make my resume appear like I had been doing the exact job the hiring manager was looking to fill. I reviewed job ads, looking for key words and phrases. I identified the key skills, experiences and capabilities they were searching for, and highlighted them in my resume – several times. I wanted the hiring manager to read through my resume and say, "Oh my goodness – this guy has been doing exactly the job we are hiring for – get him in here for an interview!"

I couldn't lie – I had to have the experiences, skills and capabilities they were seeking. When I didn't have all the elements a company was seeking, I merely highlighted the aspects I *did* have. This effort, and it was effort, yielded outstanding results for me … and it will for you too! I discuss this at great length in *The Perfect Resume*.

Another key to my success in getting interviews with my resumes was that I was mindful that most of the jobs for which I applied must first make it through the screening of applications software. Applications software is used by many companies today as a means of weeding through the hundreds of resumes they receive for their openings.

Don't believe that? Where I work, over the past year, we have averaged 157 applicants for every job opening we have. And that doesn't even include the thousands of applications we receive when we hire for police and firefighters. My wife is a school teacher, and several years ago her school had an opening for a first grade teacher. The principal posted the position at 8:30am. By noon there were over 300 applicants, and by the end of the day, over 400 individuals had applied. Eventually, nearly 1,000 hopeful applicants applied for the position. Unfortunately, that is not uncommon in the New Economy.

The way to beat applications software is to alter each resume to the specific job. Use the same key words used in the job ad – because those key words and phrases will likely be what the applications software is looking for. If it doesn't find them, then your resume never reaches the recruiter / hiring manager. And even though you are the most qualified candidate, you will not be considered for an interview.

When I say key words, what am I speaking about? Maybe they use the term *talent acquisition* instead of *recruiting* … then I should as well. If the job ad says they are looking for a *java developer*, be sure those words are in your resume multiple times. If you're serious about job hunting, then cast aside the belief that a squeaky-clean resume will do the job. Everyone has a squeaky-clean resume these days, and it's not enough to make you stand out above the crowd.

NETWORKING

If you go online you'll find scores of articles that tell you networking is the way to go when it comes to finding jobs. These articles opine that between 60% and 70% of all jobs are gotten through networking. They'll also tell you that 75% to 85% of jobs are never advertised.

Just prior to the 2001 recession, I accepted an early retirement package from the company for which I had worked for a little over two decades. The job I got within less than 30 days was gotten through my networks. It was never advertised other than through word of mouth. More on that in a bit. Webster's Online dictionary defines *networking* as:

> …the exchange of information or services among individuals, groups, or institutions; specifically: the cultivation of productive relationships for employment or business

I think that's a pretty good working definition of networking. What information or services are you sharing among individuals and groups? Well, you're going to let everyone you know be aware that you are looking for work, and what kind of work you are looking for. The service you'll offer in return? If you're smart, you'll offer something equally as valuable – you'll serve as a source of jobs for those with whom you are networking. Some of them will be walking in your shoes today…others may not tread those steps for several years. Perhaps you have already helped others find work. The best networking is among friends and acquaintances who look out for one another, who work for one another to help each other achieve their goals.

When I was laid off during the Recession, I immediately began reaching out to my network. Three days after I learned of my layoff, I found myself standing in front of the men at my church, announcing to them that I had been laid off, that I was an HR professional, and was looking for a director or VP of HR opportunity. I shared with them my experience, education and background. It only took about thirty seconds, but from that half minute I received a number of job leads, networking relationships and introductions. Those who had no job leads for me often reached out over the ensuing months to see how my search was going, and to provide encouragement to me.

As I mentioned above, during the 2001 recession, I chose to leave my company after 22 years. A few days after I made my decision, I began putting the word out. At church, I was speaking with a small group of friends and let them know of my decision to leave my company. I asked them to keep me in mind if an HR opportunity crossed their desk.

A week later, one of my friends from that small group, an attorney, called me, and the conversation went something like this:

> Troy: "Dan, didn't you say you were looking for a job?"

> Me: "Absolutely."

> Troy: "And what did you say you did?"

> Me: "I am a Human Resources professional."

> Troy: "That's what I thought. The Director of Human Resources at my law firm just announced he was leaving. Are you interested?"

Me: "Yes indeed. I would love to work for your firm, and I have the experience to do that job."

He agreed to contact the hiring manager about me and see if she would accept my resume. A day or two later he called back to say she would accept my resume.

I interviewed a few days later and was offered the job. I started within just a few days of my departure from my former company.

After I started with the firm, I asked the hiring manager why she had hired me. She said, "Well, your resume was a good one, and you had good experience. But had Troy not recommended you, I would not have invited you in for an interview because you had no law firm experience. But we trust Troy, and his recommendation swayed us to decide to interview you."

And with that, I began a wonderful ten-year career with a large law firm – all because a member of my network remembered I was looking for a job, contacted me about it, and then went the extra mile and put in a good word for me.

How can you go about letting your network know that you are looking for a job? Here's what I recommend: Identify all your friends and acquaintances who might be in a position to know of jobs that might be available. Once you have identified them, reach out and let them know you're looking for work, what kind of work you are qualified to do, and a little about your background, education, etc.

I started with my social media contacts. In addition to my LinkedIn network, I went through the address book in my e-mail and Facebook, and identified another two hundred individuals. Among them were friends, neighbors, former work acquaintances (including a number at my former firm), fellow church members, vendors who had called on me, etc. I developed an e-mail list with all their e-mail addresses, then I sent them the following e-mail:

Subject: A little assistance please!

Greetings,

As some of you may know, the law firm I have been at for the past decade has outsourced my role, so I am actively seeking a position at another firm or company. You are receiving this e-mail because you are someone I know and trust, and I am hoping you will assist me. As you know, most positions in today's work environment are gotten through networking. It occurred to me that all of you know far more people and have many more contacts in companies than I could ever possibly have, and that's where I need your assistance.

Periodically, I will send you a list of companies to which I have applied. Applying to companies today is generally through a faceless website that then scrubs your resume for key words. If you have the right key words, and the right number of them, your resume is forwarded to the hiring manager. If you do not have the specific key words, even though you may be the best qualified applicant, your resume may never be forwarded to a hiring manager.

And that's where you come in. If you know someone at one of the companies at which I have applied, a kind word to your contact on my behalf might enable my resume to reach them – or they might be willing to call my resume to the attention of the hiring manager. Or – even though they have my resume, it may be in a stack of 100s of resumes. Your support might be just the motivation for the hiring manager to seek and review my resume, especially if you attach my resume for them to review (I have attached my resume for your review and forwarding if you feel it appropriate).

I promise future e-mails will be much shorter, consisting mainly of the list of companies to which I have recently applied.
While you have my resume, let me share a few highlights:

– I am seeking a senior HR position (Director or VP)

– I have 20 years of progressively more responsible HR experience

– I have an MBA

– I am SPHR certified (sort of like a CPA designation for accountants)

If you have questions, please ask away. You may contact me at wdanielquillen@gmail.com or 303-555-1212.

Thanks for your assistance and consideration!

Daniel Quillen

Responses were immediate from many of those to whom I sent the e-mail. I received many well wishes, and more than a few job leads from that initial e-mail. What's more, I now had 450 people in the business world keeping their eyes open for positions that might be appropriate for me.

SET A SCHEDULE

I'm not going to lie to you – job hunting can get old really fast. Especially if you're not getting the interviews you had hoped, at the pace you had hoped. But you have to persevere. If you take a day or two off from your job search, before you know it, a week has passed, and you have done nothing productive to move your job search forward. Too soon, that week can turn into a couple weeks with little or no productive job search work being done. That's not a good way to conduct your job search! There are a number of elements to a successful job search, and if you set up a schedule with these elements, you can mix and match to your heart's content. Here are some essential elements to include in your schedule:

- Review job boards

- Submit applications / resumes

- Network

- Research companies

- Prepare for interviews

Let's talk about each of those elements:

Review job boards. We're all familiar with electronic job boards – places where companies place job ads. Statistics will tell you that these are not the best places to find and acquire jobs – various surveys place the number at between 6% and 15% of jobs being located and obtained through job boards. But you should not ignore them! Especially if you combine their use with other tools, such as networking. During my job search during the Recession, I used many job boards. I kept track of the number of jobs I located on those job boards, and the number of interviews I got from each board. The best job boards I worked with were:

- Ladders.com

- Indeed.com

- Careerbuilder.com

- Monster.com

TheLadders.com is a subscription site, and since you are unemployed and need to watch your expenses closely, you should weigh the value of subscribing. It is primarily focused on jobs that pay $100k or more, so if you are just starting out your career, this may be a website and expense you don't take on. When I was unemployed, I was hesitating subscribing to Ladders, and then spoke with a friend who had recently finished a successful job hunt. I expressed my concerns about signing up for a subscription that would cost me $20 a month. He helped me put it in perspective: he said to me, "Dan, you're looking for a job that pays over $100,000. Don't you think $20 or $25 per month is a pretty decent investment?" When viewed from that perspective, I decided he was right, and I subscribed. I was impressed with their website and the jobs I was able to locate there. During my search, I was able to interview for 24% of the jobs for which I applied through TheLadders.com.

Near the end of my job search, I ran across **Indeed.com**, and it quickly became my favorite job search website. Indeed.com is the kind of website I like to call an *aggregator* – they troll other job sites, company job sites, etc., and aggregate (collect, gather) all the jobs they find on those sites into one place – very helpful for job seekers.

If you are looking for entry-level or early career websites, two of the best websites out there are **Craigslist** and **Jobing.com**. In addition to early career websites, they are also a good source for blue-collar jobs. While writing this book, I went to both of those websites, and here's a sample of the kinds of jobs I found there:

- Accounts payable clerks

- Bookkeepers

- Admin assistants

- Executive assistants

- Mechanics

- Construction workers (sheet rock, concrete, roofers, etc.)

- Receptionist

- Assistant managers

- Sales (tons of these!)

- HR professionals – all levels

- Recruiters

- Staff Accountants

- Etc.

Note that several of the jobs listed (staff accountant, HR generalists, etc.) were more than entry level, so you may want to include Craigslist in your job search as well.

One of the job boards that was a pleasant surprise for me was **Monster.com**. My perception-from-a-distance was that it was a big ol' board that got lots of traffic and was very popular with job seekers. But I found seven jobs that were of interest to me, and was able to land interviews with four of them – a 57% average – not bad.

Don't overlook industry websites as well: Just prior to my Recession-era job search, my most recent ten years of HR experience was in the legal industry, so I made certain I included several websites that represented law firms. I used one national website and several local websites. If you are not aware of websites specific to your industry, there are several ways you can discover them. The first is to Google them. Go to the Google *Search* box and type: *(your industry) job websites*. Also, ask industry colleagues what websites they recommend.

Submit applications / resumes. No matter what else you do in your job search, if you're not submitting applications / resumes, you're not likely to get an interview. This is something you want to focus on.

And let me warn you – if you haven't looked for work in the last few years, this is an area that has changed immensely. The vast majority of your applications will be submitted through applications software, and it will take generally from twenty minutes to an hour to submit for each job. Most can be done within twenty to thirty minutes, but there are a few that seem to string you along, and along and along. But you have to pay attention and dot all the "eyes" and cross all the Ts.

Network. At church, I have been asked to work with those who are unemployed, and try to help them find work. The folks I have worked with are a good representation of the American public, and my conclusion is that many Americans are not comfortable networking. Whether it's this discomfort or a lack of knowledge about how to network, I am not sure. I suspect it's about equal dollops of both.

When you include networking in your daily schedule, I am talking about a number of things. First of all, you should expand your network – find people you can let know that you are looking for work. These can be fellow church members, neighbors, landlords, former work associates – at your most recent employer as well as previous. Don't forget college and even high school friends. Sure – it may have been awhile for some of us, but with Facebook, you may be connected to some of those folks who would be willing to assist with your job search. LinkedIn is a great networking website that you should avail yourself of as job searcher.

You should set aside time each day to contact members of your network to assist you with your job search. Perhaps it's an e-mail listing the companies you have applied to – does anyone in your network either work there or know someone that does? If they do, would they be willing to put a good word in for you with the hiring manager or internal recruiter? Might they feel comfortable hand-carrying your resume to the hiring manager?

Even if none of the individuals in your network has connections at the companies where you have applied or have an interview, your e-mail will serve to remind them that you are looking, and the kind of work you are looking for.

> **Let people know – a lot of people! – that I am looking for a job.**

NETWORKING GROUPS

In my job search, I discovered there were a number of networking groups that assisted me in my hunt. Each had strengths and weaknesses. Following are several types of networking groups you may consider to assist you in your efforts to end your unemployment.

Unemployment Groups. The first group I joined after my job loss was a group consisting solely of job seekers. The group was sponsored by the Economic Development Council (EDC) of the county in which I live. They did a very nice job of providing resources for job seekers – computer labs for accessing the Internet to hunt for jobs, experts to review and critique your resume, seminars on a wide range of topics – interviewing, resumes, researching companies, dealing with family issues that grow out of unemployment, etc.

The first day I attended one of their weekly sessions, I found about 50 or 60 job seekers. The director of the group (an EDC employee), asked me and two other new attendees to introduce ourselves. He asked us to provide a "me-in-30-seconds" spiel – who we were, what our educational and work background was, and what kind of employment we were seeking. When it came my turn, I said something like:

> Hi, my name is Dan Quillen. I was recently laid off from my position as the Director of Human Resources at one of the largest law firms in Colorado. I have nearly 20 years of progressively more responsible Human Resources experience. I also have an MBA and am SPHR certified – sort of a CPA for Human Resources professionals. I am seeking a position as a Director or Vice President of Human Resources.

After the three of us introduced ourselves, the facilitator asked three of the existing group members to introduce themselves. Here's basically how each person began:

> Hi, my name is Rob Smith. I am in hotel and resort management, and I have been out of work for three years…

> Hi, I am Elaine Smith, and I am a legal secretary. I have been looking for work for about eighteen months…

> I am Andrew Webb, and I am an accountant. I have worked a couple of short contract assignments, but have been looking for something permanent for a little over two years now…

Wow. I attended this group within a week of my layoff, and let me tell you – that was a sobering introduction to job hunting during the Great Recession! What happened next, and was repeated over the following weeks I was part of this group, was nearly as concerning, however. After the group settled in, the facilitator asked who in the group had interviews during the past week. Out of 50+ people, only three had been fortunate enough to land interviews! I was to learn that was not uncommon – whenever we met, we typically had three, four or very occasionally five individuals who had found interviews since the last time we met.

In fact, after the first few weeks of attending this group, I began reporting two, three, and sometimes four interviews each week. The group was amazed, and they asked how I was getting so many interviews. The Director of the EDC pulled me aside one day and asked me to prepare a presentation for the networking group about how to get interviews.

The following week, along with the two interviews I told them I had since we last met, I presented to the group. They wanted to know what "magic" I was using!

The magic was quite frankly based on three keys:

1. I was getting the word out among my network;

2. I kept the pipeline filled with resumes / job applications – I submitted resumes for130 jobs in four months – about eight to ten jobs each week;

3. And, most important of the three keys – I tailored my resume to nearly every job for which I applied.

After my presentation, several of the members of the group gathered around to ask me questions. One of them enthusiastically opined, "You should write a book about finding work during the Recession!" I thought "Why not? I write books." And that was the genesis of my first job-search book, *Get a Job!*, which was followed by *The Perfect Resume* and now by this book.

This networking group was important for me on several levels. First, it helped me understand the serious situation I found myself in – many of my peers had been out of work a long time. That told me I needed to work very hard to find a job. Each meeting included a short tutorial on some topic of importance to job seekers – as mentioned before, things like resumes, interviewing tips, etc. I learned a lot from these presentations. On occasion, someone in the group would have a contact at a company where someone had interviewed or was going to interview, and that was helpful. It gave me the opportunity to encourage people at the sessions, and we bolstered one another. Sometimes one or more members of our group were emotionally down, and the group did a good job of picking one another up.

But – the group was not a dynamic place to find job leads. Occasionally, someone would say, "Hey I heard XYZ Bank is hiring for the kind of position you said you were looking for," but that was not a focus of the group. The focus was more on supporting one another and learning or honing job-search skills.

Mixed groups. The next kind of networking group I joined was one that was a combination of job seekers, business men and women who were employed and who were on the look-out to help others who were unemployed. The group met the first Tuesday of each month in the south Denver metro area at a Mexican food restaurant.

As each meeting began, each of the forty or so attendees would stand and introduce themselves. I used essentially the same "Me in 30 seconds" presentation each as I used at the other networking group I attended:

> Hi, my name is Dan Quillen. I was recently laid off from my position as the Director of Human Resources at one of the largest law firms in Colorado. I have nearly 20 years of progressively more responsible Human Resources experience. I also have an MBA and am SPHR certified – sort of a CPA for Human Resources professionals. I am seeking a position as a Director or Vice President of Human Resources.

Out of forty participants, the number of unemployed job seekers varied, but it was usually fifteen to twenty. The group was small enough that all of us introduced ourselves. A typical introduction from an individual who was employed went something like this:

> Hi – my name is Jesse Williams, and I work for Cigna Health in their accounting department. I am a Manager of Accounting there. And – Bob Smith – you said you were looking for something in logistics – I know we have some openings in that department. Let's swap contact information after the meeting today.

While networking groups such as those we've been discussing are essential to your job search, **don't forget social networking** – LinkedIn, Facebook and Twitter in particular – when it comes to networking. All these social media sites can be valuable tools in your networking / job search efforts. If you're not using any of them – you should be!

Of the three, Facebook is more of a social network than a professional, job-seeking network; for job-seeking you want **LinkedIn**. And Twitter is a short messaging service in a world of its own. However, all are still helpful tools for you. As of this writing, I have between 500 and 600 friends on Facebook (aren't I popular?!). I also have close to 600 connections on LinkedIn. That means that within seconds I can get the word out that I have lost my job and am looking for employment to roughly 1,000 people! (Note: some of my friends in Facebook are also connections on LinkedIn; however, most of my Facebook friends are social acquaintances / friends, while most of my LinkedIn conections are professional connections.) Now is not the time to be bashful or self-conscious about letting people know you are seeking work.

Now – an important thing to remember with your networking, even through social networking – is not to sound desperate in your requests for assistance. Be professional and precise about your situation. When I say precise, I don't mean:

> OMG! I just lost my job! If I don't get a job soon my babies will starve and we'll be out on the street! Please help!

Even if you're feeling that way, be judicious in what you share. Consider something more along the lines of the me-in-30-seconds I shared with you earlier in this chapter:

> To all my friends in Facebook land: This afternoon I was laid off from my position as a Mechanical Engineering associate at Engineers-R-US. I have nearly five years of progressively more responsible engineering experience. I also have a Master's degree in Computer Science to go along with my Bachelors degree in Mechanical Engineering. I am seeking a position as a Mechanical Engineer, Design Engineer or any other related jobs. If you could help me get the word out, I'd appreciate it. If you'll "Share" this (along with an encouraging word or two about me!), it will go to all your friends, and perhaps one of them will know of a job or two out there for which I am qualified.

Then, every so often, let your Facebook friends know what's going on:

> Hey all! I have an interview with Bob Jones at Acme Engineering this Friday afternoon. Wish me luck. Also, if any of you know Bob Jones or anyone else at Acme, please let me know.

If someone does contact you who knows Bob Jones, be sure and ask them to put in a good word for you with Mr. Jones before your interview.

You can do essentially the same things in LinkedIn, although I think LinkedIn is a little less informal than Facebook.

Twitter is also another of the social media options out there and is quite informal (it's difficult to be very formal when you're limited to 140 characters). To get the word out about your unemployment, perhaps your message is something like:

> Lost my job today. Seeking Mech Engnr, Design Engnr. 5 yr exp, Bach in ME, Mstrs in Comp Sci. Can u help get the word out?

A message like that gets the word out to all your tweeple, and still allows you 18 additional characters to wax eloquent!

So don't forget social networking as a useful instrument in your job search.

I joined and participated in several other groups that had various purposes / focuses. Some sought to get job seekers together with those who knew of jobs. Others provided training on a variety of topics related to job hunting.

Tell my friends, connections, and tweeple that I am looking for a new job!

It would be well worth your time to seek out and join networking groups, both those consisting primarily of job seekers as well as those consisting of a mix of job seekers and employed individuals.

Make sure, however, that you're not spending all your time networking, to the exclusion of actually submitting resumes and applications for work. It's easy to keep busy and have the illusion of searching for a job, but not actually submitting for one.

Research companies. An often over-looked job search tool is researching the companies with which you have obtained an interview. I think it is one of the most important things you can do after you have arranged an interview, and may make the difference between you and "the other guy." You should become extremely familiar with all aspects of the company. Go to their website and follow every link, read every scrap of information you can find, so that you learn all you can about the company. Read newspaper stories (easily obtained on the Internet), comments on investment websites, etc.

One of my favorite sources of information on companies is their *Annual Report*. All publically traded companies have annual reports, and most can be found online. These reports can be a gold mine of company information. They almost always have an introduction from the CEO or president of the company. They will often provide information about company strategies (e.g., expanding their European markets, focusing on the Pacific Northwest, etc.). Comments about recent mergers – or proposed mergers, recent acquisitions, divestitures, etc. are all good information to have in your back pocket as you head into your interview.

I have preached this principle many times in recent years to those with whom I have met to assist in their job searches, and I almost always follow that counsel myself. And yet, notwithstanding that, I went to a job interview after having scanned the company's website in a perfunctory manner. May I tell you my chagrin when the first question I was asked in the interview was: "What do you know about our company?" Here was an opportunity to shine by showing how informed I was about their company history, current markets, growth and strategy, etc. I failed miserably. My mind nearly went blank – because there was precious little in there about this company. I uttered a few thoughts, but even to me it sounded pretty lame. I kicked myself for the rest of the interview, and I daresay it negatively affected my performance during the rest of the time I had with the hiring manager. It was, to put it bluntly, an opportunity missed.

And I knew better! So don't find yourself in the same situation – prepare yourself. If you aren't asked, "What do you know about our company?" during the interview, you should find a way to work your knowledge in. For example, at the end of most interviews I have been on, I have been asked, "Do you have any questions for me?" This is your opportunity to show them you have an interest in the company beyond merely interviewing for a job. "Why yes, I do. In your most recent annual report I see where your CEO, Mr. Brown, said you were 'going full-speed ahead' into Europe. Will that move have any impact on the department I will be working in?"

Researching companies is something you should do once you secure an interview. I have a friend who has been out of work for awhile. He tells me he is an expert at task avoidance – finding things to do that seem to keep him busy, but in reality just keep him from productive job search activities, and researching companies is one of those areas. He will see a job that looks interesting to him, and rather than submit his application, he busies himself doing research on the company. Before he knows it, days – or even weeks – have gone by and while he knows a lot about the company, he has not applied after hours of research. So, while researching companies has its place, don't let it be a substitute for productive job searching.

Prepare for Interviews. We'll speak more about this in one of the other chapters in this book, but this is something good you can do during the day to keep yourself busy. Think of the questions you're likely to be asked, and perhaps more important, how you're going to answer those questions.

When I was looking for work, I set and followed a daily schedule. This helped me stay on task. While I didn't follow it religiously, I was pretty true to it. I changed when the situation called for it – for example, if I had an interview the next day, I might spend several hours the day before preparing for the interview – reviewing questions, researching the company, etc. Below is a sample day from my job search.

> 8:00am to 11:00am – Search job boards, apply for any jobs that are of interest.

> 11:00am to noon – research companies you have applied to. Try to find the hiring manager at the company. Company websites, calls to HR departments, networking contacts, etc. can all help with this.

Noon to 1:00pm – Lunch

1:00pm to 5:00pm – work your network; contact members of your network via e-mail or telephone. See if they know anyone at the companies where you have applied.

Feel free to shake it up a little. At the end of the day, whatever schedule you set, you should keep busy eight hours a day.

That's an important point – your job now is to find a job, and you should not spend any less time searching for work than the amount of time you previously spent on the job. Forty hours is a nice round number – that should be your target. More is better; less is not!

SET GOALS

Do you remember one of your teachers in school at some time teaching you about goals? Perhaps how to set them? I seem to remember one of my teachers saying something like "A goal not written is just a wish."

I would suggest setting job search goals for yourself that will help keep you focused and on track on your job search. For example – I have a friend who set a goal to submit at least three resumes per day. He said it was interesting – sometimes that was difficult, but because of the goal he kept working until he had found at least three jobs for which he was qualified and for which he applied. But he also said it was amazing how many times that third resume he submitted – primarily simply to meet his daily goal – yielded an interview.

If you're struggling getting in forty hours of job searching a week, then perhaps a daily goal of eight hours each day is helpful, and one that you revisit daily. If something comes up and you only get six hours on Monday, then perhaps Tuesday and Wednesday your goal becomes nine hours for each of those days.

Another goal that may help you be successful in your job search is to call X number of members of your network each day. Five? Ten? Call them, remind them you are still looking for work, and you wondered if their company had any openings in your area of expertise. As stated earlier, even if they don't know of anything, your job search is back at the top of their radar screen, and may pay dividends down the road. In addition to asking them if their company has any openings, you could also ask them if they know of someone else that would be good for you to network with. These are just a few suggestions – I am sure there are other areas you could set goals in that will help you move your job search forward, and hopefully bring it to a successful conclusion!

The things we have talked about in this chapter should help you secure that important interview.

Get That Perfect Interview checklist

_____ I need a good resume – one that provides the critical information hiring managers, recruiters and HR departments are looking for.

_____ An appealing resume is one that is aesthetically pleasing – not too cramped, limited use of paragraphs of prose, etc.

_____ I must *tailor* my resume for every job for which I am applying. One size does not *fit* all!

_____ Get the word out! Let my friends and work associates know I am looking for work, what my skills and education are, and what kinds of positions I am seeking.

_____ Align myself with networks that will help me accomplish my goals – finding work, learning how to perfect my resume, research companies, etc.

_____ Don't forget to use social networking!

_____ Set a schedule – and stick to it!

_____ My job is now is to find a job – I should work at least eight hours each day on my job search.

_____ Prepare myself for my interviews.

_____ Set goals for my job hunt – so many hours per day, a certain # of resumes submitted per day, number of networking contacts to make each day, etc.

Kinds of Interviews

If you fail to prepare, you're prepared to fail.
– Benjamin Franklin

If you have been out of the job search market for awhile, you may be unaware that there are a number of different kinds of interviews. We'll talk about several of the more common interviews you are likely to run into during your job search.

Telephone interviews. Telephone interviews are becoming more and more popular these days. As human resources departments, recruiters and hiring managers have less and less time, they turn to telephone interviews to do initial screening for candidates. Do not make the mistake of thinking your phone interview is less than a face-to-face interview! It is a legitimate interview, and one you must be prepared for. About a year before I was writing this book, we were hiring an individual where I work. The position was a six-figure professional job, and we identified half a dozen strong candidates. Some of them were in different states, so rather than flying them in, we decided to do all first interviews by telephone.

Several of us gathered in a room for the interview. We called one of the candidates. When he answered, we could hear that he was outside – the wind was blowing and we could hear it whipping against the phone's mike. We identified ourselves and asked if this was still a good time for his interview. He said: "Oh – is that now? I wasn't sure whether the interview was at your time or mine. But yeah, I guess now is fine. Just let me get into my office in the house."

Mistake #1 – not knowing the correct time for the interview.

Mistake #2 – not being in a good environment where he could take the call. (Don't worry – there are more mistakes.)

We sat in the interview room, listening to this fellow work his way from the back yard into the house, through the kitchen and into his office. Along the way, he played with the dog and chatted briefly with his wife.

Mistake #3 – he wasn't professional in his demeanor.

Finally he made it to his office. We heard him close the door and settle in at his desk. We should have known that the interview wouldn't go well, after the start we had. A few questions into the interview we asked a relatively routine question. His answer was so out in left field, we wondered if he understood the question. It was like if I asked you what the temperature was, and you answered that baseball is one of your favorite sports to watch!

We asked another question, and he didn't answer. We waited through a few moments of dead silence, and then one of us said, "Hello, are you there?" He answered, "Oh, yes I am. Sorry about that – my wife was making faces at me through the windows of my office, and I was doing the same back to her. What was the question again?"

Mistake #4 – he was an idiot…

Mistake #45– not treating his phone interview like it was a real interview.

Next candidate please!

Suffice it to say -- when you have a telephone interview, treat is as a *real* interview – because it is! Prepare for this interview as you would any other interview. Arrange the environment for the interview. I have a dog that loses her mind when someone knocks on our door or rings the doorbell. She barks incessantly and ferociously. My office is right next to the front door, so I always put her in the back yard when the time for my interview was approaching. If anyone else is home at the time of your interview, be sure and let them know you will be interviewing, and that they should be quiet and not interrupt you. If you have small children who are home, this would be a good time to arrange for a play date at another little friend's home.

Some have gone as far as to suggest you dress up for the phone interview – dress as you would if it was a face-to-face interview. I never did that, but I can see the wisdom in that. If you feel that will make you more professional in your interview, I say: "Go for it."

Telephone interviews are legitimate interviews!

Interviews with HR departments. Busy hiring managers often turn to HR departments to do the initial screening for the job they have open. Even though you are not speaking to the hiring manager, do not treat this interview lightly. In fact, it provides a different degree of difficulty than an interview with the hiring manager. HR representatives may not know the language of the job that will be filled. Think of an IT position, that has jargon and acronyms that most non-IT people don't understand. But it's not only IT jobs – virtually every job has its own language, jargon and acronyms that are understood perfectly well among professionals in the field. But – HR people may not speak that language, so be cautious as you speak with them.

Once, I was asked to write a magazine article on a very technical subject. The article was to appear in an industry magazine. My boss reviewed my first draft, and then asked me, "If you took this home to your wife, and had her read it, would she understand it?" I answered that she would not, and he said, "Then you need to rewrite this so your wife will understand it." That's been great counsel for me through the years in my writing, and I think it also applies here. Assume the HR person you are speaking with does not speak the language you speak, and make sure you are communicating well with him / her.

Interviews with recruiters. You may have an interview with internal or external recruiters. The former are employees of the company you are interviewing with, while the latter are not. Remember the same thing for recruiters as you do for HR representatives – they may not speak your language. Generally speaking, I have found that recruiters will often speak the language, but not always. The level of questions they ask you will be a clue as to how well they understand the language. Stopping occasionally to ask, "Was that answer clear, or did I get way too deep on this topic?" The last thing you want to do is have a recruiter walk away thinking, "I didn't understand a word she said!" Her report to the hiring manager will most likely not be very positive.

Team interviews. These are very popular across all industries and for about any job. One of the things hiring managers want to know is whether or not you will get along with the people with whom you will be working. Team interviews will likely consist of individuals who will be your peers at work, perhaps a direct report or two, as well as the hiring manager and one or more of her / his peers. You need to bear that in mind as you interview and answer questions. Make sure you don't alienate your potential co-workers: "Well, when I join a company, it usually takes me a short time to be the superstar in the work group." Probably not the best answer if you're looking to impress your potential co-workers!

Where I work, the last few years we have done a form of interviewing that I find unique, entertaining and one that yields a lot of information in a short amount of time. We call it Speed Interviewing, and it is patterned after speed dating. With speed interviewing, you will meet a large number of interviewers in a short amount of time. Let me give you an example:

As part of the interview process for the position I now have, I was competing against four other candidates. We arrived in a large room, where there were five tables set up, and each table had four interviewers. Each candidate sat at a separate table and participated in a team interview with the four individuals at their table. Fifteen minutes into the interview, a facilitator came by and told each of the candidates our time was up, and we moved to the next table of interviewers. So in a little over an hour (75 minutes, actually), each candidate interviewed with twenty members of the organization. Some tables were staffed by interviewers who would be direct reports, some were potential peers, and some were peers of the hiring manager. Each group of interviewers had different questions for the candidates.

After the interviews were completed, the five of us went together on a tour of the organization which was conducted by several employees.

While we were on our tour, which took an hour or so, the hiring manager and HR department were debriefing the twenty interviewers on their experience with each of the candidates – what did they like, what didn't they like, who was the strongest candidate, who should definitely be considered and who should definitely not be considered. And – the employees who conducted the tour were also asked about their impression of each of the candidates.

Our Speed Interviewing was not a replacement for a more formal interview with the hiring manager, but the input was important. It's important to note that they didn't take a vote and that was the say the "winner" was selected (although, I suppose that could happen). But I can tell you the hiring manager took seriously the input received from these interviews.

The counsel for you if you are faced with something like speed interviewing, or team interviews, or something a little different than what you might expect – be flexible. Roll with the punches. Have a good time with it.

Interviews with hiring managers. This is of course your penultimate (second-to-the-last) goal – to get an interview with the hiring manager. You've leaped all the hurdles, bridged the chasms and swam the moats keeping you from this interview. Now is not the time to blow it.

Often, the interview with the hiring manager is the last in a string of interviews (telephone interviews, interviews with recruiters / HR departments, teams of peers or direct reports, etc.) but at the end of the day, you're not going to get the job unless you interview with the decision maker – which is usually the hiring manager. S/he will certainly listen to the input from all the previous interviews, will be interested to get input from those who participated in those interviews, but at the end of the day, the hiring manager will take the flack for a poor hire. You have got to shine in this interview.

Kinds of Interviews checklist

_____ Telephone interviews are real interviews – treat them as such!

_____ Team interviews are very popular in American businesses.

_____ Watch the use of jargons and acronyms when speaking with HR representatives and recruiters.

_____ Be flexible in my interviews.

_____ Be prepared for any format when interviewing.

Kinds of Questions

You miss 100 percent of the shots you don't take.
– Wayne Gretzky

Before you begin preparing for your perfect interview, you should be aware of the kinds of questions you might run into as you head into your interview. I have grouped them into eight categories / kinds of questions:

- General questions

- Behavioral questions

- "What if?" questions

- Ability-based questions

- Problem-solving questions

- Cultural-fit questions

- Task-specific questions

- Other questions

Let's discuss each type of question briefly.

KINDS OF QUESTIONS

General / informational questions. These questions are often the first questions you'll encounter in your interviews. They include questions designed to learn a little about your professional background and experience. The interviewer may be looking for information about why you left your last job, or why your stay at a particular job was so short. Conversely – the interviewer may notice from your resume that you were with a particular company for many years, and they will be curious about why you left after so many years. Examples of general questions include:

"How long did you work at XYZ company?"

"Why did you leave this company?"

"Do you know how many others were laid off at the same time you were?"

"I see you have a gap of eleven months between these two jobs listed on your resume. What did you do during those eleven months?"

Interviewers who ask general questions are trying to learn more about the professional you, and may be asking to clear up concerns they have about your work history.

Behavioral questions. I have to admit, these are the questions I use frequently when I interview candidates, and from my experience, most other hiring managers do as well. So – expect to be asked behavioral questions. Behavioral questions seek to understand how you have reacted – behaved – in certain situations in the past. Behavioral questions might include things like:

"Tell me about a time you had to discipline one of your employees."

"Share with me how you handled a conflict with your manager."

"Can you tell me a time you had conflicting priorities, and how you handled them?"

"What was the most difficult management decision you have ever had to make. Tell me why you made that decision."

The interviewer asks these questions to get insights into how you might handle similar situations if s/he hires you.

"What if?" questions. "What if?" questions are similar to behavioral questions, but the timing and perspective is different. While behavioral questions provide information on how you handled a particular situation in the past, "What if?" questions ask you how you would handle certain situations that might arise. I have used these questions often, and they frequently are based on situations that we have recently dealt with in our work environment. "What if?" questions might include things like:

> "How would you handle a situation where one employee is taking credit for the work her peer has done?"

> "How would you handle a phone call from the mother of an employee who wants to discuss the discipline you have recently taken against her daughter?"

> "What would you do if a customer returned a dress that had obviously been worn for longer than just to try it on?"

> "If the results of a study you are asked to perform do not support the position of your supervisor, how would you handle that?"

The interviewer is evaluating your answers to these questions to see how well you think on your feet, and whether the course of action you suggest would fit into the culture of the company with which you are applying.

Ability-based questions. These questions typically focus on the skills required to do the job for which you are interviewing. When I was in college, I interviewed for a job at a grocery store, and I remember the hiring manager asking me what the cost of one pound of strawberries would be if the cost for three pounds of strawberries was 52 cents. I remember the question because I got it wrong! (I am normally very good at doing math in my head...but not that time!) Ability-based questions might include things like:

"How many widgets per hour did you produce at your last widget factory?"

"How many words per minute can you type?"

"How good are you at using pivot tables in Excel?"

"Can you take dictation using shorthand?"

Interviewers who ask ability-based questions are trying to determine whether or not you have the skills to do the job for which they are interviewing you.

Problem-solving questions. Problem-solving questions sometime combine elements of behavioral, ability-based and "What if?" questions. The interviewer poses a problem you might be faced with while doing the job for which you are interviewing. Problem-solving questions might include questions like:

"If you were in charge of a large outdoor event and the weather forecaster on the radio says there is a 100% chance of heavy rain during most of the event, what would you do?"

"If you had to schedule all the workers for a particular shift, what information would you need to make sure you are successful in staffing the shift?"

"Your largest customer had a grand opening scheduled for next weekend, but a pipe burst and they need to move the grand opening back a week. However, all the resources you need to provide the banquet for them are already committed to another event. Both customers are extremely important to the company. How will you meet their needs?"

Interviewers who ask problem-solving questions are trying to determine how well you think on your feet, how you react to crisis or stressful situations, and whether you have the problem-solving abilities and creativity to solve the problem at hand.

Cultural-fit questions. Cultural-fit questions are similar to behavioral and ability-based questions, but are focused primarily on cultural fit. Cultural-fit questions might include questions like:

"Our corporate values are professionalism, integrity, respect and customer service. Can you tell me about a time when you demonstrated any one of those values?"

"If you knew a co-worker was stealing from the company, what would you do?"

"Are you most comfortable working in a team, or independently?"

"Describe the kind of culture you work best in."

Interviewers who ask cultural-fit questions are trying to determine whether you will fit into the company's work environment and culture. For example, in a culture that puts great value on consensus decision making and team work won't be a place that a lone wolf, individual performer is likely to feel comfortable in, nor will they succeed.

Task-specific questions. Task-specific questions could also be called by another name: Tests. Often, employers will provide opportunities for candidates to demonstrate their knowledge or abilities by accomplishing an assigned task.

A number of years ago, I managed a training center for AT&T. When it came time for me to hire a new trainer, I evaluated the resumes and selected the top half-dozen candidates. I made appointments with each of them. I instructed each of them that not only would I interview them, but that I wanted them to select a topic they would be likely to teach in the training center, and plan to make a 15-minute presentation to me. Based on my interview with them as well as the expertise they demonstrated during their presentation allowed me to see them in action and have an idea about who would perform up to the standards I expected of my instructors.

Other task-specific questions might include:

Editing an article

Troubleshooting a problem with a PC or server

Formatting and typing a business letter

Making a sales presentation

Hiring managers who ask task-specific questions / provide tests for applicants are interested in whether or not candidates can perform the job at a certain level of competence.

Other questions. You will undoubtedly encounter other than these types of questions. When you do, take a deep breath and plunge in. I once worked with a peer who was fond of asking candidates what kind of animal they were most like. Sigh… I suppose he was looking for how creative the candidates could be. Anyway – if you are a candidate who fields a question like that…play along. Other variants on the "what kind of animal are you" question are: what color best describes you, what kind of car best describes you, etc.

Seriously, other questions could come your way – just smile and make the best of them!

Kinds of Questions checklist

_____ There are a variety of kinds of questions that can be asked; be prepared for each one.

_____ Behavioral questions and "What if?" questions are popular – prepare for them!

_____ If the job I am applying for lends itself to a demonstration, be prepared to show my expertise.

_____ If I am asked what kind of animal I am, play along!

Preparing for Your Perfect Interview

*It's not the will to win that matters—everyone has that.
It's the will to prepare to win that matters.*
– Paul "Bear" Bryant

So you've landed an interview? Congratulations! You're one crucial step closer to ending your season of unemployment. But – you still have a lot of work to do to ensure that you have a successful interview. You need to do all you can to be absolutely 100% prepared for your interview. You can show up as you are, and hope for the best. Or you can prepare for the interview, and hone your answers to questions you expect to come your way. I recommend the latter approach.

When I lost my job in the midst of the Recession, I hit upon a process that I felt really improved my performance during my interviews. I highly recommend it for you.

As you prepare for the interview, let one thought become your mantra:

The interview isn't about me. It's about the company.

That may seem counter-intuitive. They called you in for an interview, didn't they? They'll be asking you questions about you. You will be answering their questions and telling them about you...When you begin thinking that way, re-frame your thoughts to:

PREPARING FOR YOUR PERFECT INTERVIEW

The interview isn't about me. It's about the company.

Recruiters are looking for candidates that will meet the needs of the companies they represent. Hiring managers are looking for someone who can do the job, will fit into their company's culture and will get along with co-workers. Every answer you provide must answer those (often unasked) questions – how do you show that you are the best candidate for the company? How do you prove to those interviewing you that you can meet their needs better than any of the other candidates?

The interview isn't about me. It's about the company.

Now that you have your new mantra in mind (*The interview isn't about me. It's about the company*), you're ready to take the next step in the preparation process.

My new mantra: *The interview isn't about me. It's about the company.*

A few days before your interview, find some place quiet where you can think and ponder about your upcoming interview. Have a pen or pencil and paper with you, or if you work well in front of the computer, make that happen.

As you think about the interview, think of the questions you expect to be asked during your interview. Put yourself in the place of the hiring manager, recruiter or HR representative. If you were one of those people, what questions would you ask? What concerns might you have about yourself as a candidate?

Start first with your resume. Look it over from top to bottom. Since you followed my counsel and tailored your resume to this particular job (see the *How to Get That Interview* chapter), make sure you have a copy of that resume. Go through it closely – look for things in your resume that might stimulate certain questions. If there are things on your resume that might cause a question or two...

...write down those questions.

Don't just think about the questions – *write them down*. What kinds of questions might your resume cause to come to the mind of your interviewer? Remember – put yourself in the shoes of the interviewer and determine what they might want to know.

Did you stay a short time at your last job? Expect a question about that; and *write it down*. Are you likely to have less experience than other candidates? Expect a question about that; and *write it down*.

After you have exhausted all the questions you can think of that will come from your resume, move next to the job description / job ad of the job for which you will be interviewing. Focus first on the requirements you read in the job ad. How do you stack up against the requirements for the position? What questions might be asked of you as they relate to the position? If you were the hiring manager, what questions would you ask a candidate for this position?

Remember the last chapter, where we talked about the kinds of questions you are likely to run into during your interview? As a refresher, here is the list again:

- General questions

- Behavioral questions

- "What if?" questions

- Ability-based questions

- Problem-solving questions

- Cultural-fit questions

- Task-specific questions

- Other questions

Think of questions that might be asked from each of those categories and…write them down!

Once you have identified and written down all the questions you think you'll be asked, then – **and this is important** – *write down the answers*! This is the time to do that, when there is no pressure on you. Think each question through, think about the best answer possible, and write it down. Don't just think it out, but write it out. This gives you the opportunity to work out sentences and present your answer in the most powerful way possible.

Be honest in your answers. Also – look for ways you can answer the question that will make your hiring manager realize you would bring a lot of value to their company if they hire you. Remember:

…write down those questions and their answers.

Let's spend a little time on this part of your assignment. While I was writing this book, I went to a job board (it happened to be Monster.com) and queried for jobs in Electrical Engineering. Here was the first ad I reviewed (the company name has been changed):

ELECTRICAL ENGINEER
ABC Company manufactures Geothermal and Watersource heat pumps in a 128,000 sq ft facility in Fort Lauderdale Florida. The site manufactures ultra high efficient HVAC equipment, including residential and large commercial units. Our manufacturing processes go beyond industry standards as we continually improve our processes to assure the highest level of quality including the shortest lead-times in the industry. By choice, we are committed to a diverse workforce - EOE/Protected Veteran/Disabled

Responsibilities
• Design and develop Water source heat pump electrical and electronics controls.

• Develops wiring diagrams and harness assembly drawings for particular product lines.

• Develop and coordinate with technical documentation team for controls product information and technical documents.

• Collaborate and help produce engineering specifications and design of heat pump unit controls, electrical wiring harness and electrical box.

• Able to work in a dynamic engineering and manufacturing environment.

Required competencies and qualifications
1. Bachelor's degree in Electrical Engineering (BSEE) or equivalent.

2. Minimum 3 years of HVAC controls related experience, including troubleshooting and diagnostics of complex control applications.

3. Familiar with test languages: LabView preferred.

4. Ability to manage multiple tasks/projects simultaneously.

5. Experience with UL standards a plus.

6. Skilled in the use of standard computing tools: Microsoft Office - Word, Excel, PowerPoint, Web Browsers, Project Management, E-mail.

So, Ms. or Mr. Electrical Engineering candidate, based on this job ad, what questions do you suppose you could anticipate might be part of your interview? (Even if you're not an electrical engineering candidate, you should play along as well...)

Here are a few I came up with, based on the opening paragraph (you can't forget that!), the *Responsibilities and Competencies / Qualifications* sections:

1. Tell us about your experience working with large residential and commercial HVAC systems.

2. You may have noticed we boast some of the lowest lead times in the industry. Based on your engineering experience, what stumbling blocks do you think we had to overcome to be able to make that claim?

3. Can you speculate what industry standards we have exceeded in our HVAC equipment?

4. Have you had experience designing wiring diagrams and harness assemblies for any products? If so, please tell us about what you have done.

5. Tell us about any experience you have had working with technical documentation writers.

6. Have you produced technical documentation for any of the products you have designed? If so, tell us about that.

7. Tell us about the HVAC experience you have had in your career – equipment you worked with, designs you were primarily responsible for, etc.

8. If you ran into a situation where a prototype heat pump repeatedly overheats and shuts itself down, what steps would you take to isolate the problem?

9. Tell us about your experience with LabView.

10. If you have not used LabView, have you used similar test languages? If so, what were they?

11. Have you had the opportunity to have any of your designs UL tested? If so – what were the results?

12. Can you please describe for us the process of getting a product tested and approved by the UL certification board?

13. What was your GPA in your core engineering classes?

I am certain you can think of other questions, especially if you are an electrical engineer looking for a job. But remember – once you have written down the questions, you are only half done – you need to also answer – in writing – each question.

To give you a flavor of how to answer the questions, following are some of the questions I wrote down as part of this exercise when I was out of work. I had a rather lengthy list of these questions (about 30) I reviewed before each job interview. Initially it took me quite a bit of time to come up with the questions and then the answers, but since I wrote them down, they became a fabulous "study guide" for me before each interview. As I had additional interviews, I added questions I had been asked that weren't on my list – to my study guide. If I wasn't happy with the answers I gave during the interviews, or thought I could make them stronger, then those are the answers I included in my study guide.

The study guide I created became a valuable tool to assist me in my preparation prior to other interviews – it was easy to run down the list of questions and refresh my memory. I studied them as part of my daily schedule either the day of my interview or the day before (sometimes both), and took them with me to my interviews. Since I always arrived quite early, I took the study guide with me and studied it in the car prior to my interview. Following are a few of the questions – and answers – from my study guide:

Question: Tell me about a time when you:

1.   *…had a difficult situation with a co-worker.*

Answer: A few years ago we got a new director of legal recruiting at my firm. Andrea was a hard driving, get-it-done-at-any-cost leader. She was a tremendous recruiter, finding exceptional talent for our organization. However, sometimes, in her zeal to bring the best talent into the firm, she made offers that caused problems for the existing workforce (or more particularly, for management!). For example, at our firm, we awarded the title of Senior Associate to those attorneys who had at least five years legal experience, two of which had to be at our law firm.

To get top talent, Andrea would sometimes extend offers to experienced attorneys with the promise that they would come into the firm as a Senior Associate. Since these candidates didn't have two years experience with our firm, bringing them in as Senior Associates was unfair to experienced attorneys already at our firm who were waiting to complete two years with the firm so they could become Senior Associates.

I spoke with Andrea and listened to her reasons for wanting and needing to bring these individuals in as Senior Associates, and she had some good reasons. I explained why it was posing problems for the firm – that existing employees were upset, that her offers violated firm policy, it created inequitable situations for existing employees, etc.

As we discussed possible solutions, it was apparent to me that our existing policy made it difficult for Andrea to attract top talent to the firm. I decided it was time we overhauled our long-standing policy about requiring two years within our firm to be promoted to Senior Associate. I made a case to our Executive Committee, and the change was approved.

Debrief: Note that when I described the difficult situation. I didn't throw my co-worker under the bus – painting her as difficult to work with (which, by the way, she was!), but rather I presented her as someone passionate about her job and her drive to be successful (which, by the way, she was!). I let the hiring manager know I was flexible, open to discussion, willing to change for the right reasons. At the same time, I let the hiring manager know I felt rules and policies were important, but that the needs of the business came first, and I was willing to make changes if necessary.

2. …*wrote a report that was well received.*

Answer: A couple years ago, at my recommendation, our firm competed to earn a spot in Fortune's Top 100 Companies in America to Work For. Part of the process was to have fifty percent of our randomly selected employees complete a fairly extensive survey.

We didn't win. But as part of our feedback, we were provided a synopsis of our employees' responses to the survey, categorized in about every imaginable way possible: by length of time with the firm, men / women, age, by specific minority, job family (attorney, secretary, paralegal, etc.), etc.

I wrote a multi-page report on the results of the survey. I highlighted areas the firm scored the highest, and what I thought we were doing that caused high ratings in each of those areas. I also identified the areas we were weakest, expressed my thoughts about why we were weak in those areas, and made proposals about how to strengthen those areas.

I presented the paper first to our Executive Committee and then to the firm in a Town Hall meeting. The Executive Committee expressed appreciation for the thorough presentation and boiling down the statistics into useable data. The Town Hall meeting generated tremendous discussion and great ideas on how to improve the firm.

Debrief: This answer allowed the hiring manager to see that I was proactive (I recommended that the firm participate in the contest) and had the ability to analyze and present data in a clear and concise manner.

Write down the questions I think I'll be asked, then write down the answers.

Additional questions to prepare answers for include:

Question: Tell me about a time when you:

3. …had to make a difficult decision with limited facts.

4. …when you set your sights too high (or too low!).

5. …had a new boss or co-worker whose trust you had to gain.

6. …had to deal with an angry customer.

7. …overcame a major obstacle.

8. …when you had competing priorities and not enough time to do them all. How did you solve the problem?

9. …had to resolve a conflict between two co-workers who reported to you.

10. …persuaded team members to do something your way.

11. …creatively solved a problem.

12. …anticipated potential problems and prepared for them.

13. …used good judgment to solve a major problem.

14. … took a sales area that had been under-producing and made it produce.

15. … solved a difficult personnel problem.

16. … had to discipline a problem employee.

17. …debugged a difficult software problem.

18. …managed a major construction project.

19. …were responsible for project managing a multi-million dollar project.

And so forth. Note that "Tell me about a time when you…" and "Help me understand how you handled…" questions are pretty popular now. They allow the interviewer to discern if you have had experience in the areas that are specific to a particular job, and how you handled yourself in certain situations.

You should also expect cultural-fit questions such as:

> 20. If we hire you, what kind of employee will you be for us?

> 21. If I asked the people who worked for you what kind of manager you were, what would they say?

> 22. Give me three terms that describe your management philosophy, and why.

> 23. If you owned this company, what direction would you want the company to go in?

THE MOST IMPORTANT QUESTIONS TO PREPARE FOR

As important as some of these questions are, the very most important questions for you to focus on are the questions you hope they don't ask – the ones for which you have the weakest answer. Hoping they won't ask those questions is not a good interview strategy! Now is the time to develop an answer you can live with, that will allay any (or most of the) concerns of the interviewer, when you're not on the hot seat. While those questions are probably as numerous as there are candidates – we all seem to have at least one area of weakness – here are the types of questions you should be able to answer:

> "You've been out of work for a long time. Why do you think that is?"

> "You don't have nearly as much experience as some of the other candidates for this position. Why should we hire you?"

> "Can you explain these gaps in your employment history?"

> "Why did you leave your last company after only a few months?"

These are the kinds of questions you need to be doubly prepared to answer in an interview. Preparation up front is key to surviving this mine field. Perhaps you have good answers to those questions; if that's the case, then you should work out your answers ahead of time. Perhaps your answers are less than satisfying to you; if that's the case, you need to massage them to make sure they will pass muster.

You can't lie, of course. But how do you address the question: "Why did you leave this company after only a month?" if the real answer is you got fired for poor performance?

Here are two possible answers to the above question:

Answer #1 – I was fired for poor performance.

Answer #2 – It's very hard for me to talk about this. When I took the job, it appeared to be a great fit for my skills and background. But once I got into the job, I discovered that I was in way over my head – I really didn't have the knowledge and skills necessary to do the job. That became apparent very quickly. If the company would have had time to train me or work with me, I am sure I could have come up to speed. As it was, they needed someone to be able to hit the ground running. It was a mutual decision that I leave.

What questions do I hope they won't ask?

So – which answer would you prefer giving? I know which one I would prefer hearing as a hiring manager! Even though the second answer would give me a little concern, I am by nature a pretty fair-minded person, and can see how something like that could happen.

An important concept to keep in mind is that you must sell yourself! You are the product, and the hiring manager is the customer. Look for opportunities to answer questions in the most positive, advantageous-for-the-company way possible – remember your mantra:

The interview isn't about me. It's about the company.

I had a friend who had been unemployed for several years. On paper, he looked like a great candidate – he had a Bachelors degree in electrical engineering and an MBA. He had a decade of experience in the field in which he was seeking employment. On paper, he was as good a candidate as you could hope for. He had many interviews, but was never the selected candidate.

One day after he learned he hadn't gotten yet another job, I proposed we do a mock interview. In preparation for the interview, I asked him to write down all the questions he could remember from his most recent interview as well as any others he could remember from previous interviews.

He came by my house with a fair number of questions. I told him to answer the questions as he did in the interviews, to the best of his recollection, and I started asking him the questions. The second question I asked him was:

"Have you ever used XYZ software?"

"No."

"That's it? You didn't say anything else?"

"No."

I thought I had found a clue as to why he wasn't getting any of the jobs for which he'd interviewed, so I pursued that question a little further. I asked him if he was familiar with the XYZ software, and he said yes, of course, that it was one of the more common software packages in his line of work, but that he'd never used it before. I asked if there were similar software packages that did the same thing and if he had used them. He assured me that was the case – they were critical to the achievement of the work he did. I suggested that a better answer to the XYZ software question may have been:

"No, I've not used XYZ software before, but I have used ABC and DEF software packages, which do the same thing. I am very adept at software, and there's no question in my mind that I could come up to speed on XYZ software very rapidly."

As we went through his list of questions, his responses to many of them were similar to the example I provided above. Yet, even the questions he answered positively were answered briefly and sparingly – with no effort to sell himself or his abilities.

We discussed that aspect of his interviewing, and he agreed to work on selling himself more. The key, of course, was to figure out how he could show the hiring manager that he could solve all her / his problems.

Finally, one of my favorite questions to ask candidates – usually as the last question in the interview – is:

> We have a number of excellent candidates for this position. Why should we hire you?

If you are asked this question, **this is not the time to be humble**. Tell the hiring manager what you will do for them if they hire you (remember your mantra: *The interview isn't about me. It's about the company*):

> Well, you should hire me because I am the best! You need someone to lead your HR organization, and I have been leading HR organizations for many years. I have extensive experience in benefits, compensation, recruiting and training – all areas you're concerned about. I would love to put my experience and skills to work in your organization, and I know you won't regret hiring me.

This is your opportunity to really make a statement about your strength and capabilities as a candidate. Don't hold back – you tailored your resume to the job ad to get the interview. You tailored your responses to questions to make your strengths evident to them – and those strengths were the strengths they were seeking. Blend all those to answer this question in a manner that will showcase your strengths as a way to meet their needs and solve their problems.

After all your hard work, don't wimp out and say something like, "Well, I'd really like to work here because it's a lot closer to my home."

MY LEAST-FAVORITE QUESTIONS

There are two more questions that you will almost assuredly run into if you do much interviewing. They are questions I am not fond of, but they seem almost like a rite of passage for interviewers and candidates. Those questions are:

- Tell me about your strengths, and

- Tell me about your weaknesses.

If I could ban two questions from the interview arena (aside from illegal ones, and questions that had anything to do with animals, colors, cars, etc.), it would be these two. I think they show a lack of imagination and may indicate poor interviewing skills. Alas, I can almost guarantee you will run into one or the other, if not both of these questions. So it's best to be prepared for them.

The answer to the first question – about your strengths – should be evident: your strengths just happen to be exactly what the employer is looking for! You tailored your resume to the key elements of the job and that helped you get the interview. Carry that tailoring into the interview. You can't lie, of course, but you can accentuate the positive. The job is a sales position and you've picked up during the interview or from the job description that they are especially interested in candidates who have opened new territories before? Provided you have done that before, that is one of the strengths you share:

> Well, Bob, I think one of the things that makes me stand out from other candidates is that I am really good at opening up new territories. In fact, in my last job I was so successful at doing that, that I was sort of the company pioneer – being sent ahead into new territories to open them.

They're looking for an exceptional finish carpenter? Then that's one of your strengths and one of the things you enjoy doing most.

Now, to my least favorite of these two least favorites: "Tell me about your weaknesses." For years, common counsel was to make a weakness appear to be a strength that will appeal to the employer:

> Well, I guess I tend to work too many hours – sometimes I get so caught up in the job that I spend more time at work than I probably should.

Or

> I guess I am a perfectionist, and sometimes I am not as patient with others who aren't.

Most interviewers will see through answers like those as a make-your-weakness-appear-as-a-strength tactic. I would prefer to answer the weakness question with a weakness that has nothing to do with the job for which I am applying. For example, when I was interviewing for my previous job – Division Manager of Human Resources at the City of Aurora, Colorado – had I been asked this question (I was not), I would have said something like:

> Well, I think I am a little weak in international HR. There have been periods of my career that I was really good at that, but in recent years, my skills in that area have become pretty rusty.

The City of Aurora probably has no need for international HR skills, so that weakness is pretty benign and would not concern an interviewer.

My brother-in-law asked me how to handle the weakness question if he were to run into it during an interview. He had a successful career with the Marines as a Public Relations officer, and was transitioning to private industry. Most of the jobs for which he was applying were state-side and had no need of dealing with foreign governments or non-English-speaking people. The weakness we decided he would share was:

I guess my greatest weakness is that I find it difficult to keep my train of thought and a good word flow when I am speaking through an interpreter.

So, while they may not be my favorite questions, expect to run into them during your interviews, and prepare accordingly.

DEAD MOOSE ON THE TABLE?

Do you have a dead moose on your table? Or perhaps an elephant in the room? Do you have any idea what I am talking about? If not – read on. If you do, well, read on as well. This may be one of the most important elements for preparing for an interview that no one else will ever tell you.

References to elephants and dead moose are known as euphemisms.

> Euphemism = exchanging a mild or vague phrase in the place of one that might be considered unkind, blunt or unnecessarily insensitive.

Either way, if you have a dead moose on your table as it relates to your resume or job hunt, you need to be aware of it, and address it. Ignoring the dead moose – which everyone sees and recognizes – does not make the dead moose go away; people are just polite and waltz around it, ever aware of its presence, but just not willing to address it head on.

What's the dead moose on your resume? Here are a few common ones:

- Little or no experience

- Gaps in employment

- Lack of Education

- A series of short employment opportunities

- Your age (old or young!)

Let's address of few of these more common issues that may be on your resume:

Little or no experience

Face it – the only way to get experience is to…well, get experience. You need to find someone that will give you a chance and hire you even though you do not have experience, or you have little experience compared to the other candidates with whom you are competing. But most companies aren't particularly…charitable…when it comes to hiring inexperienced workers. What to do?

And here, let me add, that lack of experience isn't just limited to young workers. You could be a stay-at-home mom re-entering the workforce after a decade or more raising your children. Or you can be a mid- or late-career worker changing fields/industries. The common thread to each of those situations is a lack of experience.

There are a couple strategies. I have walked in those no-experience shoes (all of us have!), and here's a strategy I hit upon: When I was eighteen years old, a lot of my friends were getting jobs in construction, and where I lived, those were the highest-paying jobs for young people. But my friends had an "in" – their father worked for or owned a construction company. Their neighbor owned a construction company and agreed to take them on as an apprentice. I had none of those advantages. After being turned down by construction company after construction company, I hit on a strategy. I decided to offer two strengths to the hiring manager.

First, I developed a two-part strategy. When I went for yet another interview, before we were very far into the interview, I said, "I know I do not have any construction experience. But I am a hard worker, and will give you a full day's work for a full day's pay. I am athletic and have good strength and excellent hand-eye coordination, and I am certain I will be able to come up to speed quickly." That was Part 1. Then came Part 2: I said, "I will even work for half wages until you feel I have learned enough to merit full pay." (I'll bet none of my competition offered that!)

The hiring manager – the owner of the small steel construction company with whom I was interviewing, seemed amused and intrigued. Said he: "How can I pass up an offer like that?!" And he hired me. (**Note**: notwithstanding my declaration of being willing to work for half pay, to the business owner's credit, he paid me full wages from Hour One.)

Another strategy is to focus on your strengths, not your weaknesses. But how do you do that? Rather than speak of your weaknesses – your lack of experience – trumpet your strengths. Sometimes those strengths are directly related, and sometimes you have to draw the connection for the interviewer. Perhaps you've never sold electronic equipment before (or never sold anything before), but you own nearly every electronic gadget known to man and you know how to make them work. That's the strength you share with the hiring manager: "I have never sold electronic equipment before, but I probably personally own most of the electronic equipment you sell in your store, and I know how to make it work. And – I can show others how to make each of those things work." What a great asset you would be to this store manager (remember your mantra: *The interview isn't about me. It's about the company*).

I will share one of my favorite hiring stories here, the story of a woman who was in the middle of her career and looking to change fields. I interviewed her for a position for which she had only minimal qualifications – all of the other applicants had much more experience than she did. She fared well in the interview, notwithstanding her inexperience. But to be honest, I was concerned about her lack of experience. Yet when I asked my final question, she knocked the ball out of the park. My question was, "We have a number of very qualified candidates; why should I hire you?" She straightened up in her chair, looked me in the eye, and said;

> *No one* will work as hard as I will work, and no one will be as passionate as I am about this job! I love this work and will give it my very best every day!

What's not to like about that answer?! (By the way – I hired her, and she has proven to be one of the best hires I ever made!)

In her case, the strength she had to offer was not years and years of experience – *in fact, that was the dead moose on her table* – she offered up that which she had to offer – her passion and work ethic. After all was said and done, in her case – that was enough. Perhaps it will be for you.

Sometimes, people view something about themselves as a dead moose on the table when it really is not. Or, if it is, they should do what they can to change it from a weakness to a strength. Once, I was interviewing candidates for an HR assistant position. Two of the candidates spoke with very heavy Hispanic accents. One of the women obviously felt her accent was a dead moose on her interviewing table – a weakness. She handled her weakness by apologizing repeatedly during her interview for her heavy accent.

The next woman had an equally strong Hispanic accent, but she dealt very well with it; in case we felt it was a weakness, she helped us see that it was really an asset for us: she said something like, "You've probably noticed that I have an accent. I am a native of Mexico, and Spanish is my first language. This will be a benefit to you because I can communicate well with any Spanish-speaking employees or clients that you have." What a difference in those two approaches! And – the second candidate certainly understood that the interview was about the company, not her.

Gaps in employment

> **What's the dead moose on my job-search table?**

Gaps in employment are some of the most common dead mooses on today's job seekers' tables. The New Economy has seen to that, and many hiring managers, recruiters and HR departments understand that. But you still must be prepared to address that question, for it will surely come up. As a hiring manager, I don't give candidates a pass on that, but I do ask them to explain each of their gaps in employment history.

Laid off? Tell me you were laid off, and what number or percentage of the company was affected by the layoff: "I was one of the last people hired, and when the company had to let go 20% of their customer service representatives, I was in that group because of my short tenure with them."

But if it was a one-person layoff – you – I want to know that as the hiring manager. Hopefully you'll have a good explanation for that. But don't just say you were laid off if in fact you were terminated for poor performance or some other reason. And – work out an acceptable answer when I ask the inevitable question: "Why were you let go from your previous employment?" Another tactic to address a gap in employment is to fill that gap with *something* – start your own consulting company, take temporary work through a temp agency, preferably in your area of expertise. So rather than a large gap between jobs, you can fill that time with some sort of employment. As a bonus, it will help provide a few shekels in your pocket to help make ends meet.

When I was laid off from my law firm in 2011, friends recommended that I start an HR consulting company. Had I done so, I would have shown my company as I would any other job on my resume. If this is what you choose to do, I think it is important to actually form a company (most states charge only a reasonable fee to form a company – in Colorado it is $10) and seek to obtain clients. First of all – it's the honest thing to do. And second, it will strengthen your assertion that you actually did form a company if you can say that you provided HR consulting services for a number of companies.

Forming companies isn't just for professionals like attorneys, project managers, architects, IT professionals, etc. You are a carpenter? Then form **Harvey's Handy-Man Services**. You're a car mechanic? Great – then form **Dave's Mobile Mechanic Service**. Both of these companies can get customers by advertising on Craigslist, putting flyers in supermarkets, hiring teens to deliver flyers door-to-door (or do it yourself with family members, etc.).

Do you have a friend or family member that owns a company that would give you a contract position, so that you can show that you were employed during that time? That's only an option if you actually do work for the company, but it is an option I know a number of friends and acquaintances have used. Even if it is only a few hours each week or month, you can use this on your resume.

Gaps in employment are not insurmountable, but you need to be prepared to put the best face on the situation as possible.

Lack of Education

If you have a lack of education in this market, you are fighting an uphill battle. My first counsel is: *go get that education*! There are scholarships and grants, student loans and many other sources for you to get your education. You have put it off this long, and now it is coming back to haunt you. While you are looking for work, now is a great time to go back and finish that degree you started twenty years ago. There are so many educational institutions out there that are geared toward adult education, look into them.

In the meantime, you need a job. I can tell you that the way most people who do not have their education get jobs is through networking, so be prepared to work that tool very hard during your job search.

Since many companies use applications software to screen resumes (and education is one of the quickest / easiest things they can use to cut candidate lists from hundreds to scores), you will need to find someone in your network who knows someone in the company that has the job you want. Reach out to them, explain about your lack of education, and ask them to deliver your resume to the hiring manager along with a few positive words. "Hey – I know this person who would be a great employee for our company. She doesn't have her degree, but I think she'd be a rock star for us. Would you be willing to look at her resume?"

I have been hiring people for over two decades, and as good as I am, it is still scary to hire someone from a one- or two-page resume and a 45-minute interview or two. If I can get a recommendation like the one shared above, you bet I will be willing to take a look at your resume.

This works because many job descriptions are written with an "educational escape clause," something like:

> **Education**: Bachelor's degree in Business, Communications or Marketing. *Equivalent experience may take the place of formal education.*

But – screening software is often set to screen on education, so even though there may be this experiential equivalency clause, it's just easier to screen out all those who do not have the minimum educational experience.

Reach out to your friends in person, via e-mail or through your connections, friends and tweeple on LinkedIn, Facebook and Twitter.

Lack of education adds a degree of difficulty to your job hunt, so you have to be a little more aggressive about certain aspects of your search.

Your age (old or young)

It seems that if you are young in your career, or old in your career, there is a temptation to feel like all the older / younger workers are getting the opportunities, and that because of your youth / older age you are being passed over. There are things you can do to combat these prejudices.

For younger workers, can I just assure you that if I am willing to hire someone who is just out of college, or very new in their career, I understand you won't have a lot of experience. And that's okay. But – understand that as a new college grad with no more experience than a summer internship or two, you're not going to land a vice president position at a major company! It's not because of your age – it's because of your experience, or lack thereof. You will need to be content with starting your career where most of us older folks have – at or near the bottom of the ladder. The higher-paying jobs typically require at least some experience.

If you really are after the bigger bucks, you might consider sales positions in any of a number of industries. They will often bring on new college hires who don't have much experience, and train them the way they want them to be trained.

As you interview as a younger worker, accentuate the positive – your vigor, your excitement to finally be in the work force and your passion for the area of work you have chosen (communications, marketing, construction, etc., etc.). Stress your flexibility and willingness to learn.

Don't apologize for your youthfulness and lack of experience – capitalize on it. What are some things you can capitalize on that may be of value to the employer with whom you are interviewing? If your degree is in the area for which you are interviewing – point that out! Let them know that you are so interested in Parks and Recreation that your degree is Outdoor Recreation. Tell them you enjoyed school, but you're really looking forward to getting in the real world where you can help make a difference, rather than just reading about how to make a difference. Remember – think of things that will be important to the hiring manager, not just to you!

For older workers, yes, age discrimination is alive and well. That is why it is important for you to be cautious in what you reveal on your resume. If you include the job you got right out f college, it doesn't take much of a math expert to figure out that if you worked there beginning in 1969 that you are probably a few years beyond age 40 (50…60). That's why I recommend not including jobs past ten to fifteen years ago. Don't include your college graduation dates on your resume. Once you have gotten your interview, then is the time for you to wow them with your ability, experience and capabilities.

In *Get a Job!*, I explained a situation I had to deal with. A friend pointed out that while I was getting a lot of interviews, I was not landing any of the jobs. He suggested at least part of the reason was that I was being discriminated against because of my age. He suggested a unique approach I thought was brilliant. He suggested I prepare a short conversation about my age, and in it I would seek to dispel any concerns my potential hiring manager might have about older workers. With his guidance and advice, here is what I came up with. He suggested that near the end of my interview, when asked if I had any questions, or wanted to share anything with them, that I roll out my prepared comments. Here's what I said:

As you may have noticed, I am not a spring chicken, and I am probably older than most of the other applicants. But I want you to know that I have a lot of runway left on my career – I am not considering retirement any time soon. I have three children who are in college for a number more years, and besides, I am nowhere near being ready to retire.

(That dispels their concern that I will retire as soon as I get trained.)

I am very good at learning new software. I have been at this so long that I have used many different software packages, and have never had difficulties picking up new applications or software packages.

(That addresses any concerns they have about whether or not I can learn new software or work with new technology.)

I enjoy all ages of workers and work well with younger workers as well as workers my age.

(So much for the concerns about me being a grumpy old man…)

And I am very healthy. I have worked 50 hours a week for most of my career, and have no reason to expect I will work less in this position.

(And now they know I am healthy and they don't have to worry about me being sick all the time.)

In addition, the benefit to you is that you get an HR professional with years of HR experience. I have been doing HR so long, there are very few things that surprise me – I have seen it all. Because of that, I don't get too excited or agitated about anything that comes up.

(Adding a cherry on top – not only do they not have to worry about me as an older worker, but they actually benefit from it!)

For the purposes of this book, I wish I could tell you I used this approach many times. But I didn't – I used it only once. But…I am batting 1000 when using it – I got every job for which I applied when I used that dialogue.

Meet age discrimination head-on

Job Hopping

One thing hiring managers and HR professionals are wary about is a resume that has a lot of jobs in a short period of time, indicating the person may be a job hopper. You must guard against this in your career. I consider someone a potential job hopper if they have a history of staying at places less than two years. One or two of these short stops don't concern me, but if there are more than that, I do get concerned.

To get past that, if there are legitimate reasons for your departures, mention it both in your resume as well as your cover letter. I once interviewed a woman who appeared to be a job hopper. But her resume included the following comments on each of the jobs she'd had the previous few years:

- Company went through serious lay-offs, and since I was one of the last ones hired, I was one of the first to go.

- Company went out of business.

- Company moved the HR department to Illinois, and I was unwilling to move there.

- The partner for whom I was hired to work went to another firm, and he was unable to take me with him.

I checked out her story…and she was not fibbing – those things really happened at the companies she had worked for. Her job history prior to those four companies had been very strong, so I was willing to give her the benefit of the doubt.

That candidate was totally unlike another I interviewed. He had very good experience, but appeared to be a bit of a job hopper. When I asked him about it, he took me through his resume and said things like, "Well, I left this job to find myself. I toured South America for six months, and came back to the US with a new lease on life." Several other departures seemed to have good explanations, but when he told me he left another job to "find himself," I decided he wasn't the candidate for our company!

So – those are some of the more common dead mooses on tables that I have run into. Regardless of what your dead moose on the table is, you must develop a strategy on how to face it, defuse it, and even turn it into a strength, if possible. Hoping that no one will notice it, however, is *not* a good strategy!

THE UNASKED QUESTIONS

Regardless of the specific questions asked, keep one thing in mind – all the questions are designed to answer the following questions (remember your mantra: *The interview isn't about me. It's about the company*):

- Will this person add value to my organization?

- Can this candidate solve this very important problem I have at this time in my organization?

- Can this fellow help me out?

- Will this candidate fit into our culture and the team with which he or she will be working?

That pretty well distills it down.

MORE QUESTIONS

You're now at the last step in your preparation process. There is one other set of questions you should prepare: questions to ask your potential employer during the interview. Surely there are questions you will have about the job – think of around six to eight questions to ask your interviewer. Write them down and bring them with you to the interview. Some possible questions include:

- What do you expect the successful candidate to accomplish in their first six months on the job?

- What do you think are the key attributes of the candidate who will be most successful in this job?

- How many people report to this position?

• Why is this position vacant?

• When do you think you will be making a decision?

Note, by the way, that none of these questions has anything to do with benefits, vacation time, or salary. Your first interview is not the place to ask these questions. Asking those questions during the initial interview signals you are concerned about what's in it for you, not what you can do for their company (remember your mantra: *The interview isn't about me. It's about the company*).

Bring a set of questions to ask during my interview.

These questions you prepare for the interview should be written on a padfolio or pad of paper that you will be taking to your interview. Sometimes, by the time you reach the end of your interview, all of the questions you brought will have been answered through the ebb and flow and information exchange of the interview. Not to worry. When it comes time to ask the questions, scan your list and say, "You know, I had a list of questions to ask about this position, but it seems like you've already answered all of them."

If you will spend time doing and keeping in mind the things I have covered in this chapter, you will be prepared for your interview. That preparation will help you be confident as you arrive for your interview.

Preparing for Your Perfect Interview checklist

_____ Find a quiet place to consider my upcoming interview.

_____ Remember: The interview isn't about me. It's about the company.

_____ What questions do I hope the employer doesn't ask? Prepare for them.

_____ I am the product being sold – have confidence.

_____ Bring a set of six to eight questions for the interviewer(s) to the interview.

_____ Is there a dead moose or elephant on my table / in the room? Determine strategies to deal with these critters before I go to my interview!

Your Perfect Interview

Do you know what my favorite part of the game is? The opportunity to play.
– Mike Singletary

Congratulations – you've landed an interview – the next step to resolving your unemployment! Don't underestimate the importance of this accomplishment…you've just gone from perhaps 100 (200, 300) to 1 in the competition to get an interview to 1 in 6 (or 3, 4, or 5) to win the job.

But now is not the time to let up. If anything, you want to be sharper, quicker, more polished than all you have done to this point to get your interview. We'll talk about a few things that you should do to make sure you shine during your interview.

Speaking of shining – make sure you shine your shoes! Whether you are a man or a woman, and are late, mid- or early in your career, this is an important – and often overlooked – chore that should be attended to. And women – be sure and look at the back of your shoes – right above the heel. I have seen many women whose shoes looked fine until they turned around, and then it looked like their shoes had never been polished. And while it's true that first impressions are important, you don't want the last impression of your interview to be less than impressive!

THE 20-20-20 RULE
If you read *Get a Job!*, you'll be familiar with this next few paragraphs. When interviewing, remember the **20-20-20 Rule**:

- The first twenty feet

- The first twenty seconds

- The first twenty words

Let's discuss each of those elements:

The first twenty feet. What happens during the first twenty feet? To begin with, you are establishing the first impression for all who meet you. Here are a few first-impression things I can think of:

- You're on time (or not).

- You smile pleasantly.

- You are dressed appropriately for your interview – suit and tie, slacks, tie and sports coat, conservative dress / blouse and skirt, etc. And of course, your shoes are shined!

It is difficult to under-estimate the value of those first twenty feet – with the receptionist, the HR person or the hiring manager. Don't under-estimate the power of that first twenty feet.

The first twenty seconds. Those first twenty seconds are crucial in establishing your credibility and making that good first impression. It includes:

- You greet the executive assistant or HR specialist professionally and politely.

- You sit like a professional (not sprawled on the couch, not reclining in a chair, etc.)

- You seem calm, cool and collected.

- You shake hands firmly.

- You make eye contact and smile at all those you meet.

These physical aspects of your first twenty seconds are crucial to establishing yourself as a professional. And please understand – whether you are applying for a "professional" position or a blue collar position, or something in between, hiring managers want someone they can trust and depend on, someone who takes their job seriously. And fair or not, they will use that first twenty seconds to size you up against an invisible yardstick.

The first twenty words. Time to open your mouth and make a good impression with your future hiring manager.

- Your greeting is genuine and sincere.
- You remember – and use – people's names.
- You appear calm, your speech isn't overly informal, and you seem like a pleasant person.

So – pay attention to the first twenty feet, seconds and words.

Following are a few pointers gleaned through years of interviewing candidates for positions, and from working with hiring managers and human resources departments.

DRESS FOR SUCCESS!

You've come so far – congratulations on earning an interview! Now don't blow it by wearing the wrong wardrobe to the interview! Be sure you dress appropriately for the company and the job.

When you go to a job interview, you have one chance to make a good first impression. Before you say a word, your potential employer is already sizing you up – drawing his or her conclusions about you – and how you are dressed sends a powerful message. Are you dressed professionally, or are you dressed too casually for the position and/or the culture of the company? Is your clothing crisp and clean, or wrinkled and worn out? Do you project a professional image, or not? Sharp or dull? Poised or nervous?

Not everyone needs to – or should – wear a suit and a tie, or a skirt, blouse and ny-lons to an interview. Some places that would be clearly out of place. A construction company, for example, may think it odd that you arrive dressed in a three-piece suit to apply for a laborer's job. My rule of thumb is to dress at least one or two notches above what you expect to find in the workplace. Blue jeans and t-shirts are the ac-cepted office apparel? Then I would opt to wear a pair of clean and well-pressed khakis and a collared shirt. If business casual is the dress code (khakis and collared shirts), I suggest you wear a pair of slacks, a white or light blue shirt and a tie. Per-haps even a sports coat.

Let me share a short vignette I shared in *Get a Job!* about the absolute *necessity* of dressing appropriately for job interviews. A friend of mine was working with a Public Relations executive as his job coach. The PR guy had several interviews with a dot.com-type software company for a six-figure position. Finally the call he was hoping for came: the CEO wanted to have lunch with him at an upscale restaurant. He was excited for the opportunity and knew he was on the threshold of ending his unemployment and going to work for a premier company.

Because he felt the work environment at the company was pretty casual, he had worn slacks, a sports coat and tie to both of his previous interviews. None of the managers with whom he interviewed wore ties – they were dressed in khakis and collared shirts. So in this, he followed my rule of thumb – he dressed a level above the expected workplace dress (although, I have to admit – I probably would have worn a suit and tie). For his meeting with the CEO, he had decided to dress like the company's managers – business casual. But he was uncertain enough about his decision that he called my friend to get his input. My friend strongly recommended he dress a notch higher – not a notch lower – than what he had worn during his interview with the company's managers – in other words, he was recommending that the candidate wear his interview suit. They discussed and debated the issue at length, but the more my friend recommended a suit, the more firm the candidate became in his position of dressing more casually. He did agree to wear a tie, which he felt was a huge concession.

The day of the lunch interview finally came. The candidate got to the restaurant early and waited excitedly for the CEO to arrive. Imagine his shock – and discomfort – when the CEO walked through the restaurant doors wearing an expensive suit, gleaming white shirt and conservative red tie! When they shook hands, the candidate noticed expensive gold cuff links on the CEO's monogrammed shirt sleeves. They exchanged small talk on the way to their table. Once settled, the following conversation ensued:

> CEO: "I reviewed your resume and was very impressed with your education and experience. My managers spoke highly of your professionalism and capabilities. I know how PR executives are always concerned with appearances, so I wanted to show you how much I respected you as a candidate by wearing my best suit for our meeting today."

> The candidate knew he was toast. Thinking quickly, he said, "Well, thank you – you are most kind to say that. I know your company has a business casual dress code, so I dressed this way so I wouldn't make you feel uncomfortable. It seems we out-guessed one another!"

Nice try. The PR candidate didn't get the job, most likely because he made the wrong wardrobe decision.

Personally, I would prefer to risk being a little overdressed to being dressed too casually for an interview.

Just to drive home my point, can you take one more story about dressing appropriately for a positon? A year or so before I wrote this book, we were hiring for a managerial position. The salary range for the position was $85,000 to $117,000. Imagine our dismay when one of our candidates showed up dressed in tennis shoes, blue jeans, a t-shirt and a hoodie. When we told him we had decided not to interview him, he was astounded. When he asked why, we told him he didn't dress appropriately for the interview, and we therefore questioned his judgment.

LOCATION

This may seem ridiculous to mention, but be sure you know where you are going for your interview. When I was in high school and college, when I asked a girl on a date, if I didn't know precisely where she lived I always did a trial run before our date, making sure I could find her home, how long it took to get there, etc. I also did a trial run to the restauruant or activity we were headed for, just to make sure we didn't get lost or were late. (Yes, I know – perhaps my OCD is showing a bit.)

And so you should do when you have gotten an interview. Make sure you have the address of the company. In addition to knowing what time to be there, know well *where* you are to be – what building, what floor, who to ask for, etc. The day or two before your interview, drive by the building. When I was unemployed, I was excited about a job interview I had with Western Union. I MapQuested the address, and felt confident I could find the place.

The morning of the interview, I arrived, as usual, quite early for the interview. But I was concerned to see that the address I was given had about eight or nine buildings associated with it – it was a campus layout! I was glad I had arrived early – I was able to go to the front desk and ask where I should be for my interview. But – it would have been better to do a trial run a few days in advance.

When I interviewed with the law firm I worked at prior to my layoff, their offices were located in downtown Denver, on the 41st floor. The day before the interview, I drove downtown in rush-hour traffic (since my interview was the next day at 8:30am), found where to park, and then walked into the building. I took the elevator to the 41st floor. I timed all this, and from leaving my driveway to arriving at the 41st floor, it took me 55 minutes – so basically an hour.

The next day, I left my house at 6:30am – two hours before my interview. Since traffic wasn't quite as busy as the day before (since I left an hour earlier!), I got there in plenty of time – I had about an hour and fifteen minutes to burn before the interview.

Fortunately, I had brought my behavior-based questions with me, so I used the time to bone up on my answers and to practice them. I also had the job description, so I could refresh my memory about all the elements of my specialty they were looking for.

As the time for my interview approached, I left my car and walked to the building. I waited in the lobby the last ten minutes or so, then at about five minutes before my interview, I stepped on the elevator. I arrived at the reception desk about three minutes before my interview, and informed the receptionist I was there, and who I was to interview with.

TIMING

Now, as you read that last few paragraphs, you might be thinking, "Dan's OCD is showing again!" And yes, you would be correct. But beyond that, I cannot stress enough **the importance of being on time to your interview**! Notice I said, "On time," not "Arrive early." I have to be honest, it annoys me to no end to have a candidate show up twenty or thirty minutes before the time for their interview. Often, I schedule interviews back to back. That means if you arrive twenty minutes early and my secretary calls me, you are interrupting someone else's interview. Also, even if I am not in an interview, believe me, I have plenty to do. I will not appreciate that you have arrived early. It does not signal to me your eagerness about the job – it mostly just annoys me. And it is never good to annoy the hiring manager.

As bad as arriving early, arriving late is worse. Through the years, I have had far too many candidates arrive late. Sometimes they call ahead to tell me they are stuck in traffic, or have gotten lost, or whatever. That softens the blow a bit, but it is not impressive. You see above how fixated I am about time. The fact that you are late may throw other interviews off. Or – I may interview you for half an hour instead of 45 minutes or an hour – I will short you, not the candidate after you.

If you are late for an interview, you have one strike against you before you even meet the hiring manager. If you arrive really early (ten to thirty minutes) you have about three quarters of a strike against you before you begin.

For those times when you are unavoidably late, it is good to have the company's main number as well as the number for the hiring manager with you the day of the interview. If you are running late, by all means call the hiring manager. But he or she may not be in their office – they may have other meetings, be interviewing other candidates, etc. If no one answers his or her phone, try hitting 0 and # during their voice mail message – that will often transfer you to the hiring manager's secretary, who can get a message to the manager. If 0 # doesn't work, having the main number of the company allows you to reach the receptionist, who can then get you to the manager's secretary.

But bottom line is – don't be late. You've heard the axiom *Better late than never?* Well, when it comes to interviewing, I would say: *Better never late.*

Don't be late for my job interview!

BRING YOUR RESUME

Before you leave for your interview, you would be wise to print a half dozen copies of your resume. Team interviews are very popular these days, and you may find yourself interviewing with a panel of employees, or you may go from one interview to another. Bringing extra copies of our resume shows how professional you are, how prepared you are for your interview.

If you have one, use a padfolio to carry your extra resume copies. That will keep them looking fresh and professional. If you don't have a padfolio, a pad of paper would be sufficient – just tuck the copies of your resume after the last page. The padfolio / pad of paper also has the benefit of being something you can take notes on during your interview. This isn't a must, but I always like to interview candidates who take notes during interviews. We all like to think what we are saying is important or of interest to others.

Bringing copies of your resume serves a number of purposes. First, one of the things I like to ask candidates to do is to take me through their resume, highlighting their primary responsibilities. I may ask a variety of questions, including why they left, what they liked most / least about each job they held, and perhaps what their greatest accomplishment was at each job. It is a lot easier to do that if you have copies of your resume in front of you. If there are multiple team members in the interview, you'll be able to make certain each member of the team has their own copy as well. I think bringing extra copies of your resume helps project and form the image you want – that of a professional who is courteous and thinks of others, and is always prepared. Portraying yourself in that manner is worth the price of a few pieces of paper with ink on them (your resume!).

Whether you need them or not, I think it is a good sign of your preparation and professionalism if you arrive with resumes ready for your interviewers.

BUSINESS CARDS

Whenever you interview, you should always ask for the business cards of those with whom you are interviewing. When you receive them, first of all – look at them – look at the names on them. This serves several purposes – first of all, it helps you make certain you get everyone's names correct – did she say Cassie or Cathy? Tris or Chris? Bob or Rob? That is essential because people's names are important to them…and getting them correct is something you want to do during your interview: "Thanks, Kathy, that's an interesting question," or, "As Rob mentioned earlier in the interview,…"

IT'S ABOUT THE COMPANY

Now is a good time to remind you of your new mantra – the one you and I developed together in the last chapter:

The interview isn't about me. It's about the company.

It was good to keep your new mantra in mind as you prepared for your interview, and it is doubly important to remember it now. Everything in the interview is about the company. As we discussed earlier, you may have been thinking it's all about you. That makes sense – they called you, asked to interview with you, they have your resume and application. But believe me, it is all about the company, not all about you. Your interviewers will be evaluating your answers against what their needs are. These are the questions they may be seeking answers to:

- How will you help us solve our problems?

- What will you do to boost our sales?

- How will you enhance our customer service?

- What will you do to protect our company against lawuits?

- Will you fit into our culture, and into the personality of our team?

- And other questions like these.

They will most likely *not* ask you those specific questions (although they may ask some of them). But they will be listening carefully to what you say and trying to determine if you are the answer to their problems. So remember that.

Let me give you an example that happened while I was writing this book. We were interviewing candidates for an important managerial position. We asked the candidate to:

Tell us why you would like us to hire you for this position.

The candidate, who had impressed us greatly on earlier interviews, said something like: "I'd love to work for the city of Aurora because having a job here would cut my commute in half. That's more time for me to spend with my family."

Now, there's nothing wrong with spending time with your family, but with an answer like that she missed a golden opportunity to establish herself as the best candidate for our organization. Compare that answer to this one:

I have always admired your company, and when I read the job description, I realized I have skills and abilities that will help you meet your strategic goals this year.

Or this answer:

> Well, I read in the newspaper that you were expecting to bid on some new government contracts over the next few months. I have great strengths in that area, and thought my experience in that area would be able to help you immediately.

Now in the case of the candidate we were interviewing for the managerial position, that portion of her answer was less than impressive. But she saved it a bit by adding:

> In addition, I was raised in Aurora, and even though I no longer live here, I have a great connecton to the city. I would welcome the opportunity to serve the community in which I grew up and where I graduated high school.

The second part of her answer was much stronger than the first part.

THE INTERVIEW

Often, as a warm-up question, interviewers will ask the softball (easy) question, "Can you tell us a little about yourself?" I think this is sort of an ice breaker, an opportunity to put you at ease. It is important to note that in response to this inquiry, most interviewers don't want to hear about your spouse, children, sports activities, hobbies, etc. They are really looking for how you can help them. Remember that – no matter how nice they are (and they may really be nice people!), what they are really looking for is whether or not you can add value to the organization, solve a problem for them or help them out in some way. All your answers should be given with those things in mind.

You can use this question to answer those unasked questions, and to set the tone for the rest of your interview. I have been asked that question before, and here is my answer:

> First of all – thank you for your time today. I know you are all very busy. In answer to your question: I am an HR professional with nearly two decades of HR experience. I have a broad range of skills, from legal compliance, employee benefits, succession planning, and organizational development.

(**Note**: each of those are elements from the job description, or at least those elements I am experienced in). I am passionate about HR – I love the legal and formal aspects of HR, but I also enjoy the opportunity to touch people's lives and make a difference. I've worked for Fortune 20 companies and small organizations, and feel comfortable in both settings. And that's me in a nutshell.

Look at what I just told them about me in about thirty seconds:

- I am an HR professional;

- I have nearly twenty years' experience;

- My skills range covers the areas they are looking for in the job;

- I love the technical and legal aspects of HR;

- But I also love the people aspects of HR;

- I have worked in large and small organizations and enjoy both;

- I can be succinct and get to the point.

And – did my questions answer any of the following unasked questions:

- Will this person add value to my organization?

- Can this candidate solve this very important problem I have at this time in my organization?

- Can this fellow help me out?

- Will this candidate fit into our culture and the team with which he or she will be working?

I think my answer addressed each of those questions in one way or another. And if not exactly, I am sure it came a lot closer than if I had told them about my hobbies (genealogy and writing), the recent trip I took to Ireland, my children's accomplishments (I have a long list!), etc.

Answering that question in that manner also gives you a connection with your interviewers. As they ask you other questions, they can refer back to your opening remarks: "Dan, at the outset, you said you had experience with legal compliance. Can you tell us a little more about that – what were your specific responsibilities in that area?"

A question like that, by the way, tells you a little about what's on their mind – what kind of things keep them awake at night, problems they hope you will help them solve.

Here are a few important things to keep in mind during your interview:

Listen. Dring your interview, you have the opportunity to show the interviewer(s) how good a listener you are. Be sure to allow the interviewer to ask all of his/her question. Don't be in such a hurry to answer the question that you cut the questioner off mid-question. First of all, it's rude. Secondly, you may answer the wrong question, because you thought you knew where the person was going with the question. I had experience with that when I was helping my boss interview a woman who we eventually hired. She was so anxious to answer questions, that she leapt in before the questioner was completely finished. I had reservations about her as a candidate, but overall liked the package she brought to the table – she had the skills and abilities to really help us, notwithstanding this issue. After we hired her, guess what we discovered? She wasn't a very good listener.

Sometimes you are asked a question that you simply don't understand. I would suggest not trying to answer what you *think* you were being asked – if you do that, the risk there is that you'll answer something totally unrelated to what the questioner meant. If you don't understand the question, say so, and ask them to repeat it. Something like: "I'm sorry, but I don't understand exactly what you're looking for. Can you please restate your question?"

DANGEROUS QUESTIONS

There are questions you must watch out for, questions that may pose problems for you. No, they aren't necessarily the questions that highlight your areas of weakness – we talked in an earlier chapter about how to prepare for and answer those questions. The questions I am speaking about are those that may inadvertently show things you don't want hiring managers to see. Questions like:

"Tell us about a time you didn't get along with a co-worker."

When answering this question, don't throw your co-worker under the bus. If you do, it may signal to the hiring manager that you are difficult to work with, or not a team player. Focus on the positive things you did to get through the situation without damaging the relationship – we discussed that in the previous chapter. If the situation that comes to mind is really a negative one that puts you in a bad light no matter how you portray it, then select another situation where you and a co-worker didn't get along. If you have worked long enough, you probably have any number of examples from which you can draw, and of course, if you have prepared for this question, you'll have just the right answer to that question.

"Tell us why you left your previous employment."

While writing this book, I was part of a team interviewing a fellow for an important position at the city where I work. We asked him a similar question: "Tell us why you would leave your current employer to come work for us."

His answer was startling – he went on for a couple minutes about how bad his current employer was, that they didn't really have a vision for what could be done with the organization he was in, etc. In another recent interview, a member of the interview team I was part of asked this question, and we were stunned to hear the candidate go on and on about the terrible, illegal things her boss was doing. If that wasn't enough, she went into great detail about a disciplinary meeting she was called into and the reasons she was being disciplined. Turns out, she didn't care for the way her supervisor handled the disciplinary meeting. Next candidate please!

When answering questions about why you left – or are willing to leave – former employment, this is not the time to share what an idiot or jerk your former boss was, or the poor benefits package the company offered, even if those things are true. Another question I have run across often in the work place is:

"Tell us what you would do during the first six months you are here."

This is a great opportunity to share how hard you'll work, how committed to learning the organization you are, etc. It is not a time to point out the errors you think they have as an organization (even if they have expressed concern about the way they do some things). I interviewed a fellow once who basically trashed our company's compensation policy and told me how he would "clean things up" if he was to come to our company. He was not hired.

YOUR END-OF-INTERVIEW QUESTIONS

At the end of the interview, hiring managers will often ask if you have any questions. Now is the time to ask the questions you have already written down (in your padfolio or on a pad of paper) and brought with you to the meeting.

There are several reasons to write your questions down. First, during the stress or adrenaline rush of the interview, you may forget what those excellent questions were that you prepared before the interview. Second, I am generally a little put off by candidates who say, "No, I can't think of any questions for you." Really? You're not the least bit curious about this or that aspect of the job?

Often, during the course of the interview, many – or even all – your well-planned questions will be answered. That's okay; but if you have written down your questions, you can scan the questions on your pad of paper (letting the hiring manager know you really did put some thought into this interview) and say something like, "Well, I had a whole list of questions to ask you, but throughout our interview, you have answered all of them." However – you'll almost always have one question:

• *What are the next steps?*

This gives you the opportunity to find out where the company is in their hiring process, and when you might expect to hear back from them. Perhaps you are the first interview, or the last. Regardless, you should be able to learn when they will get back with you – whether for good or ill. It also provides you the opportunity to contact them if you do not hear back from them within a reasonable timeframe.

Through the years, several candidates have tried a "trial close" on me. By that, I mean they asked me something like: "Can you tell me how I stack up against your other candidates?" or "After what you've seen today during our interview, do you feel I am your top candidate?" While as a former salesman, I appreciate this, as a hiring manager I am not a big fan of it. It puts me on the spot, and I don't care for that. Having said that, I know a number of individuals whom I respect greatly, who use this tactic and have had good results with it through the years. It's just not for me.

AFTER THE INTERVIEW

Congratulations – you survived! Breathe a sigh of relief. Now the waiting begins.

One of the first things you should do is sit down and write a Thank-You note to all those with whom you interviewed. (That's another reason to get business cards during the interview.) Some experts say this is another time for you to make your case as the best candidate. However, I think it should be short and to the point, something along the lines of:

> Dear Mr. Johnson,
>
> Just a quick note to thank you for your time today. I know you are busy, and I appreciated the time you spent with me to help me learn more about Acme Engineering.
>
> Thank you so much for your time and consideration. If I can answer any further questions for you, please don't hesitate to contact me.
>
> Best Regards,
>
> Daniel Quillen

This should be written on a professional-looking Thank-you card. And remember what your mother always said – "Use your best penmanship."

When I have mentioned this tactic to people with whom I am counseling about job hunting, invariably some ask, "Won't an e-mail be easier and just as effective?" The answer is yes and no. Yes, it's easier; no, it's not more effective. Anyone can take twenty seconds and fire off an e-mail, but a handwritten thank-you note separates you from the crowd. I'd guess about 30% of the candidates I have interviewed through the years have sent an e-mail thank you, but only 1% or 2% have sent a handwritten note. It's impressive to me. Will it make the difference? Not if you don't have the skills and qualifications required for the job. But if it's close between you and someone else, who knows? I don't think it hurts.

You might also contact those whose names you have provided as references, and let them know they may be contacted. Tell them about the job for which you have interviewed, and if you want them to accentuate anything about you as a candidate, ask them to mention that if they are so inclined.

FOLLOW-UP

If you don't hear something right away, when is it too soon to follow up? Part of that depends on what the next steps were going to be for the hiring manager. If s/he told you that you were one of the first to be interviewed and it would take a couple weeks to get through the rest of the candidates, don't be calling a week after the interview.

If, however, the hiring manager told you that you were one of the last interviews, and they should make a decision by the end of the week, then I think you can call on Tuesday of the following week if you haven't heard anything. Tuesday isn't pushy – calling the Friday the hiring manager said they would make the decision seems pushy to me. When you call on Tuesday, your message should be something like:

> Hello, Mr. Johnson, Dan Quillen here. I remember you mentioned you
> were hoping to make your decision on the HR Director position by last

Friday, so I thought I would follow up to see if you have any further questions for me. Also, I just wanted to let you know I am still very interested in the position.

I can tell you from personal hiring experience that I am often unable to make a hiring decision in the timeframes I initially shared with candidates. Work gets busy, a candidate cancels and has to reschedule, and any number of other reasons.

But here's something to remember – just because getting hired by that company is at the top of your importance list, chances are pretty good that it gets easily supplanted in the hiring manager's business life – filling the position is the smoke on the horizon, and while that's important, the fire at his feet is going to take precedence every time.

Having said that, I think it's okay to check in occasionally until you're told someone else has the job (or until you get the job), but be careful – persistence is good – it shows you are interested in the job. But there is a fine line between persistence and stalking.

Don't be a stalker!

If the manager seems evasive or quits returning your calls, assume the worst and move on. You might be pleasantly surprised, and s/he may call later than you expect to offer the job, or call you in for another interview, but don't make a nuisance of yourself.

If the call comes and – sad day – you are not the chosen candidate, be professional in your response. Don't subject the caller to a litany of questions about why you weren't chosen. It is okay to express disappointment, but be completely professional. More than once I have hired someone who didn't work out, and I went to Candidate #2, sometimes just a few days later, but also as much as a few months later.

Recently, we interviewed a group of individuals for an important executive position at our city. We had a tough choice to make between the top three candidates. We finally settled on one of the candidates. When I called Candidates 2 and 3 to tell them they weren't chosen, Candidate #2 was so annoyed at not being chosen that he hung up on me! Two weeks later, the chosen candidate called us the Friday before he was to start work to inform us that he had been offered another position and he wouldn't be starting the following Monday. Guess which of the previous candidates I did not call to ask to come back in for another interview!?

It's easy to be professional when the breaks are going your way; however, the mark of a true professional is how they handle disappointment. Handle any disappointments you receive with grace and dignity.

Your Perfect Interview checklist

_____ Remember the 20-20-20 Rule – the first twenty feet, first twenty seconds, first twenty words.

_____ Dress appropriately for my interview!

_____ Know exactly where the location of my interview is. Do a trial run. Arrive early!

_____ When I arrive early, use the time before the interview to study the questions and answers I worked up.

_____ Don't show up for the interview more than about five minutes early!

_____ Bring half a dozen copies of my resume.

_____ Ask interviewers for their business cards.

_____ Remember my new mantra: *The interview isn't about me. It's about the company*. Answer all questions accordingly.

_____ Be prepared for dangerous questions – the questions I hope don't get asked.

_____ Formulate and bring at least a half dozen questions I can ask about the company, the job expectations, etc.

_____ Send *Thank You* cards to all with whom I interview.

_____ Follow up with a phone call to show my continuing interest, but don't become a stalker!

_____ If I am not chosen for the position, be pleasant, polite and professional.

9 Dressing for the Perfect Interview

If you can't be better than your competition, just dress better.
– Anna Wintour

Many years ago I read a *Peanuts* cartoon that featured Charlie Brown and his friend Linus van Pelt. Charlie Brown observes Linus's shiny, recently polished shoes, then notes that they are only shined in the front, and that the back of his shoes were not polished. When he asks Linus about it, Linus says: "I care about what people think of me when I enter a room. I don't care what they think when I leave."

I agree with Linus on how important first impressions are, but I have to disagree with Linus (and his creator, Charles M. Schultz) that lasting impressions are not as important. From head to toe, you have to be concerned with the appearance you project when you arrive for your interview (and when you leave!).

But first, you may ask:

> "Is what I wear to an interview really that important? I mean, what they are really looking for are my skills, personality, capabilities, etc. Right? If I don't dress appropriately, is it possible that I won't get the job?"

My answer(s) to that question are: "Yes." "No." "Well, maybe." Let me explain.

The answer is: "Yes." Remember back in the *Your Perfect Interview* chapter, I told the story of the fellow who showed up for an interview for a six-figure job dressed in a t-shirt, jeans, a hoodie and tennis shoes? We didn't even interview him because of the poor judgment he demonstrated in his choice of interview clothing. So in this case, the candidate didn't get the job because of the way he was dressed.

The answer is: "No." I have another example, though not as extreme, which supports my "No" answer. Where I work, we were hiring for a director position – a job with a salary well into six figures. We were working with a recruiter, and he brought us five candidates. We had invited the candidates in for a series of interviews over the course of two days. The day of the first interview arrived, and each candidate arrived and was very professionally dressed – suits, crisp white or blue shirts with spit-shined shoes. Except one. He showed up in slacks, a shirt and tie. No jacket, and his shirt was pretty…informal (although he did have a tie).

I pulled the recruiter aside and asked him if he had any concerns about the way the five candidates were dressed. He agreed that "Bob" was not dressed appropriately for the interview. The next day, Bob arrived at our offices for his interview dressed in slacks, a shirt and tie – and a jacket. After the interviews, we ended up hiring Bob, and he has been a fabulous hire for us.

Had Bob not worn a jacket that second day, would we have passed on him as a candidate? Probably not – he was head and shoulders above the other candidates who interviewed for the job. But it was a risky thing for him to have come to the interview dressed as he did. (Note – in Bob's defense, he was living and working in Arizona, and the job he was interviewing for with us was in Colorado. What he wore may have been more than appropriate for an interview in Arizona, but not quite so appropriate in Colorado.)

The answer is: "Well, maybe." I don't have a specific example to support this answer, other than to refer you to the previous few paragraphs. We hired Bob, who wasn't dressed quite appropriately, because he was head and shoulders above his competition. But – speaking of body parts – what if he had been neck-and-neck with another candidate who was dressed appropriately? It is possible that the other candidate may have "nosed" him out simply because of their respective choices of dress.

Why take the chance?

If someone in your network works at the company where you are interviewing, ask them what the hiring manager with whom you will be interviewing is likely to be wearing. Then dress appropriately. Remember my rule of thumb from a few chapters ago – dress at least one or two notches above what you expect to find in the workplace. When in doubt, over-dress!

It should go without saying (but I will say it anyway) that whatever you wear should be clean and freshly pressed. I love the look and feel of a heavily starched shirt fresh from the cleaners, but I understand that's not for everyone. But you should make sure your shirt is freshly pressed, your tie is clean and conservative (no ties with cartoon characters, beer products, political messages, etc.!) and your slacks should be neatly pressed. Speaking personally, I have to be careful that my slacks / suit pants aren't wrinkled. I always pay attention to my shirts, but sometimes I am embarrassed at how my pants look. Remember – your shirt hangs on you most of the time, but you sit on your pants. Wrinkles form at the back of the knees (remember Charlie Brown and Linus) – so take an extra moment or two and make sure your pants look fine for your first as well as your last impression!

Don't risk losing a job because you didn't dress appropriately, or because your clothing isn't clean and smartly pressed.

Shine my shoes – front AND back!

Dressing for the Perfect Interview checklist

_____ First impressions are important, but don't ignore all impressions!

_____ Dress a notch or two above the dress I expect to find in the work place.

THE PERFECT INTERVIEW

_____ It's better to be a little over-dressed than under-dressed in an interview.

_____ Be sure my interview clothes are clean and freshly pressed.

10 I am Getting Interviews ... but no Job!

I've learned that something constructive comes from every defeat.
– Tom Landry

Well, congratulations on getting interviews. As I've mentioned before in this book, without interviews, you aren't going to be landing any jobs. If you are getting interviews, then your resume must be pretty good – the competition out there is often pretty steep for opportunities.

Also, if it's just one or two interviews you've had and you're not getting the job – well, I wouldn't push the panic button yet. (Actually – even if you've had many interviews and no job – don't push the panic button – we seldom make right decisions when we are panicky!) Here are a couple thoughts:

First, I am a firm believer that everything happens for a reason, and in my own case, if I didn't get the job I interviewed for, I just chalked it up to experience and knew that something better for me was just around the corner.

But if you are getting interviews and no job offers, it's good to step back and study the situation – take inventory, so to speak. In the first place, were you qualified for the job? Most likely you were, or else you wouldn't have been invited in to interview. But if you didn't have all the qualifications necessary, you may not have gotten the job because a candidate who had all the qualifications interviewed. Was it a position you really wanted, or was it one you just interviewed for because you were out of work and needed a job? If the latter is the case, then perhaps your attitude showed through during the interview. Or maybe you reminded the hiring manager of her ex-husband, and there is no way you were going to get that job!

If none of those things happened, then review in your mind how the last interview went. Did you feel good about it? Did you walk away feeling you nailed it, that there was nothing in the interview you would have done differently, no answer you wish you could change, even a little bit? If that's the case, then you probably did fine even though you didn't get the job. Perhaps there was an internal candidate who did well in her interview, and even though you interviewed well, the hiring manager gave the nod to her. Internal promotions (or lack thereof!) send powerful messages throughout an organization. Or maybe the hiring manager didn't feel you were a fit for the team she had in place, and for the needs s/he felt the team had.

Where I currently work, we were recently hiring for a mid-level manager with a lot of responsibility. As it was a bit of a niche area of our organization, we were worried we might not get any qualified candidates. We were pleasantly surprised to receive the resumes of a number of excellent candidates. We selected five and invited them in for interviews.

Through the interview process, it became clear that one of the candidates was too junior for the position. But the other four candidates were exceptional, and any one of them could have done the job and done it well – they were all well-qualified for the position. After a great deal of soul searching, interview-note reviewing and pondering, we settled on one particular candidate because we felt like her personality and approach were more in line with what the team needed. So that "fit" thing really is important out there.

If after reviewing your performance in your last interview, you feel something was lacking, what was it? Did they throw questions at you that you weren't prepared for, and in retrospect you wish you had answered some of the questions differently? If so, then write them down in your study guide and write out the answers until you are happy with your response.

If you didn't create a study guide for yourself, kindly return to the *Preparing for Your Perfect Interview* chapter and review the counsel I gave there to think about all the questions you were likely to be asked and *write them down*. And – add the questions that stumped you in your last interview to your newly created study guide.

Did you remember your new mantra? If not – kindly return (again!) to the *Preparing for Your Perfect Interview* chapter and refresh your memory on what your new mantra should be:

The interview isn't about me. It's about the company.

Reflect on the answers you gave during the interview – were any of them more about you than about the company? Did you show how you could solve the company's problems?

Here's something to bear in mind when you are interviewing: this is a sales call. You are the sales rep, and you are selling a product – you! If you're not sold on the product yourself, you will have a difficult time selling your client (the hiring manager) on the product (yourself). Be proud of your product. Accentuate the positive, downplay the negative. Look for ways to make yourself valuable to the hiring manager and her / his company. Here's an example of how to make yourself valuable to an organization: When I was out of work during the recession, I was interviewing for a high-level position at a company that had experienced a number of layoffs through the years. That meant to me that the remaining employees were probably doing the work that others used to do. When they asked me in the interview to describe my management style, I was sure to mention that I wasn't afraid to get my hands dirty by doing whatever needed to be done, whether it was in my job description or not. I saw immediate approval in the eyes of those who were interviewing me – they weren't looking for a manager that was aloof and stayed out of the fray, so to speak, but they wanted and needed someone who was willing to wade into the situation and work shoulder-to-shoulder on issues and problems.

Perhaps your problem is *glossophobia* – the fear of public speaking. And an interview is a very personal form of public speaking. Statistics show about 10% of the population love speaking in public. Another 10% are terrified of public speaking. Are you in that latter group? If you are – you have to get over it, at least to the degree that you can perform well during a 45-minute interview.

You would never dream of making a 45-minute presentation without preparing yourself thoroughly – reading lots of source materials, making notes, forming your key concepts, etc. And – practicing your presentation in front of the mirror, or perhaps even delivering it to your spouse or significant other. Why would you do anything different as you prepare for an interview?

Through the years, I have done countless mock interviews with friends, acquaintances, even family members. Together we discuss the key points they want to make, and review the questions they think they'll be asked. Then I conducted the interview as though I was the hiring manager, and they participated as though they were the candidate. Sometimes when we came to a portion of the interview that seemed to be particularly difficult or bumpy, we would stop, debrief it, and try again. We repeated the process until even the toughest questions could be handled with grace and aplomb.

If you feel less-than-enthusiastic about your performance at interviews, or find yourself dreading an upcoming interview, perhaps a mock interview or two would help you deal with the butterflies, and help you feel confident as you head into your interview.

If at all possible, I suggest you find a professional person to help you and engage in mock interviews with you. It would be ideal to find someone who is or has been a hiring manager – they can give you real-time tips and assistance as you practice together in your mock interview. Generally, I don't suggest a parent, spouse, significant other or adult child to assist in your mock interviews. If they are the only ones available, then okay – use their assistance. But typically they won't be as critical as someone who is more objective will be, and you need someone to be a little critical, someone who can point out nervous habits: do you pop your knuckles when you're nervous, or perhaps lose or avoid eye contact? If so – you want someone to point those things out to you, and to allow you to practice your interview until those habits disappear.

Prepare. Practice. Consider a mock interview.

I am Getting Interviews…But No Job! checklist

_____ Self-introspection following an interview is important.

_____ I am a sales person, and I am also the product. Be proud of my product – sell it well!

_____ Prepare for my 45-minute interview as I would for a 45-minute presentation.

_____ Mock interviews are a valuable tool to assist me in becoming comfortable in the art of interviewing.

_____ Find someone – preferably a professional person – who can help me with my interview skills.

11   **I am Just Not Getting Any Interviews**

Just keep going. Everybody gets better if they keep at it.
-- Ted Williams

The other side of the coin from the previous chapter – where you may have been getting interviews but no job offers – is that you are sending out resumes and inputting applications and not getting any interviews.

There may be any number of reasons why this is happening, and I will share my thoughts on a couple of the more common areas, and ways to improve your chances:

- Number of candidates

- Minimum qualifications

- Your resume

- Lack of Networking

- Applications software

Number of candidates. The reason for your difficulties in getting an interview could be as simple as you are one of many who is applying for a given position. As I mentioned earlier in this book, where I currently work, over the past year we averaged 157 applicants per job opening…and that doesn't include the 2,500 to 3,000 applicants for our Police or Fire openings! And our experience is common in the employment world right now, so you need to find a strategy that will help you climb to the top of the heap of candidates.

There are a couple strategies for overcoming this situation. First, apply early. This means you must be constantly looking at and reviewing job boards. As soon as a new job comes open for which you are qualified – get your resume in! I have a friend that will see a job posted and mull it over for a few days (or even weeks) before he decides to apply. Why wait?! Unless you are blessed with the riches of having more jobs to apply for than you have time, why wait to apply?

I have a staff of five HR generalists where I work. While our average applicant pool is 157, some jobs have 400 or more applicants. To be timely in our hiring, those five people (who screened nearly 300 jobs last year) do not have time to review every single resume. (Do the math – 300 jobs times 157 applications per job = 47,100 resumes, or 9,420 resumes per screener!) So we screen resumes in the order they were received until we find enough qualified candidates to interview, then we stop reviewing resumes. If none of those candidates is hired, then we begin screening resumes again where we left off until we find another qualified batch of candidates. So, if you're applicant number 173, even though you might be the most qualified person who responds to the job posting, the chances your resume will be reviewed are slim to none. So the moral of that story is – be vigilant in your job search, and apply as soon as you see a job you think you may be interested in, and for which you meet the minimum qualifications.

Speaking of **minimum qualifications**, if you do not meet minimum qualifications, your resume may never even reach a screener, or if it does, it may be discarded quickly. If the job ad says you must have a Bachelors degree, a very quick way to cull resumes is to put all those that do not list a Bachelors degree in the "No interest" pile. Sometimes that decision is made by applications software, and other times it is made by a screener / recruiter.

How do you get around that stumbling block? Let's say you have found the perfect position for which you can do everything, but you don't meet some minimum qualification – education, years of experience, etc. To get an interview, you may need to work a little harder. Contact your network (LinkedIn is a great place to begin) and see if anyone you know works at that company. If you find someone who works there, or is connected (LinkedIn lingo) with someone who works there, see if they would be willing to make an introduction for you. They can speak with the hiring manager or recruiter and see if they would be willing to review your resume even though you don't meet the minimum qualifications. At the same time, they can tell the hiring manager / recruiter that you are a hard worker, have impeccable ethics and would be a great employee for the company to have on their team. As a hiring manager, those attributes often trump technical or job-specific skills for me.

If you do not know someone who has a colleague at the company with which you are interviewing, locate the hiring manager yourself. Go on the Internet, or call the company and ask who the manager of the XYZ (Purchasing, Logistics, Accounting, etc.) department is. Then contact the hiring manager and present your case – you have the required skills and knowledge, are a hard worker, great ethics, will not be an HR problem for them, etc., and even though you don't meet the minimum educational qualifications, you hope s/he'll consider you. It's a little more work, but what have you got to lose (other than the job if you don't try this tactic!).

Your resume. Without knowing you, I am going to make a wild guess, and say you are not tailoring your resume to each specific job for which you apply. If I am mistaken, then I apologize. But if that really is the case, kindly turn back to the *Preparing for the Perfect Interview* chapter and review the information about the importance of tailoring your resume. If you're not doing that, you're probably trying to put so much in your resume that it will apply to every job out there. That simply doesn't work in the New Economy – the skills and experience you have that relate to the job for which you are applying gets lost amidst all the other skills and experiences you load into the interview.

If you aren't convinced after re-reading the *Preparing for the Perfect Resume* chapter, then perhaps you'll want to pick up a copy of *The Perfect Resume* and read a little more about it!

Lack of networking. If you are not getting interviews with the applications and resumes you are submitting, perhaps you need to shift your focus to your network. These are the people who you know who may know hiring managers or recruiters, and can help you short-cut the process. As discussed above, these individuals can be of great value to you in your job hunt, and can provide an introduction that may make the difference between continuing to be unemployed and landing that Perfect Job.

Remember – tailor my resume for every job!

Applications software. If you are seeking interviews in this day and age, you will most likely come face-to-face with applications software. With over-burdened hiring managers and Human Resources departments and an over-abundance of candidates for each opening, employers have turned to applications software to help cull out the least-desirable applications and resumes.

They base their decision process on things like education, years of experience, and certain key words. This helps them thin the herd, so to speak. So as we discussed earlier in the book, you need to be sure and have a plan for how to address those stumbling blocks.

But that's not the point I want to make about applications software.

> • If you are fortunate enough to get past the applications software gatekeeper (ie – you have the education, years of experience and/or key words that are being scanned for), it is imperative that you follow the directions in the application software. Not doing so may squelch your opportunity to earn an interview.

> • For example, if they ask you to describe your experience in such-and-such an industry or discipline, and it says "Do not simply cut and paste from your resume," then don't cut and paste from your resume! That is something that annoys the screeners where I work to no end, and is a sure way to have your application rejected. And yet, candidate after candidate has done that.

Often, application software will ask applicants to expand on their skills or experience in a particular area. If you run into that, rejoice! Here's your opportunity to really make your case as the best candidate for the position. Don't throw this opportunity away. I can't tell you how many candidates wasted that opportunity through the years by entering only the briefest of information when they had the opportunity to wax eloquent about their skills, ability and experience.

There could be many reasons why you are not getting interviews, but those discussed in this chapter are some of the more common.

I am Just Not Getting any Interviews checklist

_____ Remember that I may be one of many candidates.

_____ Be vigilant in seeking newly posted jobs and apply immediately.

_____ If I don't have the minimum qualifications for a job, I will most likely need to employ other tools such as networking.

_____ I need to believe what this guy says – I need to tailor my resume for every job!

_____ Follow the directions in the applications software.

_____ If given the opportunity, I should provide detailed information about my skills and experience – don't skimp on the information I provide.

How to Ruin an Interview

Make sure your worst enemy doesn't live between your own two ears.
– Laird Hamilton

Okay – we've come a long way, you and I, if you have read from the beginning to this point. I have given you my thoughts and advice, suggestions and recommendations for being successful in obtaining an interview and then successfully interviewing.

This chapter contains information you'll need if you want to ruin your interview. Epic fail. Fall flat on your face. Crash and burn. Go into a death spiral. All of these are things I have experienced with candidates who have attempted to interview with me for positions I had open. Learn from their mistakes. Don't repeat them. They are not in any particular order – they are randomly provided with no nod to their incompetence or stupidity.

LIE

If you're anxious to fail in your interview, be sure and lie. The grander the lie, the better. Your lie doesn't have to be just in the interview – you can start on your resume. Don't be honest about the jobs you've had – especially your title and the dates you were in the position. Count on the fact that your employer won't check out what you've said.

It's always impressive when an interviewer doesn't remember what university s/he went to. Their resume says University of Colorado – Denver, but in their interview they say they graduated from Denver University (they are very different universities). That's a fine way to flub an interview.

Also – be sure and "puff" your resume and your explanation of what you did in a particular job. This is doubly impressive. I once interviewed a woman for a particular position. To hear her tell it, she had been responsible for some major projects – *exactly* what we were looking for. We were fooled and hired her, but in very short order, we discovered that she hadn't *led* the large projects she had told us about… in fact, as it turns out, her role in the projects had been very low level and compartmentalized. Not only did she leave the job she had for ours, she now she has to explain a very short stay at our company when she interviews for other jobs.

So – if you want to ruin your interview, try lying.

BE LATE

You doubtless recall my obsession with time, especially when it comes to candidates for jobs. It's really impressive when you show up late for an interview. You don't want to make the hiring manager think you have your hopes set on this position, after all.

While being late for an interview isn't the kiss of death, it is a warm hug. So if you want to start the interview off on the wrong foot, then arrive late – the later the better.

BE A STALKER

I have to admit, this isn't a common interview-ruining tactic, but it is an interesting one. I know a fellow who was desperate for a job. He thought it would reflect well on his research skills if he researched the managers he learned would be interviewing him, and then dazzled them with all that he knew about them. Not so much. They were pretty put off that he knew their political affiliations, the church one of them went to, the names of their spouses and at least a few of their children.

While I am certain the interviewing managers were impressed with his research skills, they were just a little unnerved by learning all he knew about each of them. Definitely an interview-scuttling move.

BE VAGUE OR EVASIVE

A definite way to undermine an interview is to strive for vagueness. This is definitely a successful tactic for trashing an interview. It is particularly effective with behavioral questions:

> "Tell us about a time when you fixed a peanut butter and jelly sandwich."
> "You know, I'm glad you asked that. I've always felt peanut butter is a great food product."

> "…Yes, but can you tell us about a time you used it to make a peanut butter and jelly sandwich?"

> "Ah – jelly, of course I forgot about the jelly. I prefer jelly over jam – don't you? I just don't like the seeds that usually accompany jams. But yes, peanut butter and jelly sandwiches are great. But don't even get me started on tuna sandwiches – to die for!"

CHEW GUM DURING YOUR INTERVIEW

This is one of my favorite activities for candidates – gum chewing. I don't believe chewing gum is appropriate in many settings – job interviews, operas, church, etc. But if you are striving to really submarine your interview, chomp away.

Be vague … and fail at your interview.

READ FROM YOUR NOTES

I have to admit that this has only happened once during an interview that I have conducted, but if you wish to learn how to really turn off an interviewer, read on. As I mentioned during the *Preparing for Your Perfect Interview* chapter, an excellent way to prepare for an interview is to write down all the questions you think you may get during your upcoming interview, then write the answers to those questions. Not only does it cause you to sit and think about the questions and work out the best answer, it will help you be confident when you are in your interview. It also provides a nice study guide as you prepare for subsequent interviews, especially if you update it with questions from interviews you have. I always take the document to interviews with me – since I arrive early to my appointments, it gives me something worthwhile to review prior to going in.

But leave your study guide in the car!

A year or so before writing this book, I was interviewing a gentleman for a very high-level HR position. At the outset of the meeting, he asked if he could take notes, and of course I said that was fine. All was going well until I asked him a certain question. He flipped open his notebook and began paging through it, scanning it for something. Finally, he found what he was looking for – the answer to my question. He then proceeded to *read* the answer to me! To add to this bizarre interview twist, he wasn't a particularly smooth reader. This happened several times during the interview, and was not very impressive. Suffice it to say we did not offer him the job.

So if your goal is to ruin an interview, this would be a unique, memorable and interesting way to do so.

MAKE ASSIGNMENTS TO YOUR INTERVIEWER

Not long ago, I encountered an individual in a setting outside work. She was a presenter at a conference, and very impressive. She and I struck up a conversation, and I made a mental note that she might make an excellent candidate for a position I would have open soon. When the position was opened, I contacted her and she was interested in the position. We set a date for the interview about ten days out.

Imagine my surprise that during that ten-day window, this woman was constantly calling and leaving me messages, assigning me tasks she'd like me to accomplish:

1. "Hello Dan, this is Norma. Please send me your company's HR strategy."

2. "Hi Dan, Norma again. Send me a copy of your mission, vision and values statements for the HR organization as well as for your company. You do have them, I assume."

3. "Dan, Norma again. I am curious about your budget and where you spend the most money in the HR organization. Please send me a copy of last year's final budget."

And so on. I suppose she was trying to show me that she was a savvy business woman who wanted to hit the ground running. What it said to me was that if I hired her, I would be hiring someone who was good at delegating up. I have enough work on my plate already, thank you. Next candidate, please!

But it's a superb tactic to ruin an interview before you even walk in the room!

BE A STORY TELLER!

Aren't story teller's grand? It's wonderful to sit around a campfire and have someone real off wonderful legend after fable after true story.

But if you want to crash and burn in your interview, be a story teller.

Sigh…I would be less than honest if I didn't admit that I have probably turned off more than one interviewer because I was a story teller. Sometimes, if someone asks me what time it is, I find myself compelled to tell the history of clock making, and sometimes forget to get around to telling the questioner what time it is!

If you find yourself providing long answers (setting the stage, so to speak), and suddenly realize you can't recall what the question was – you are probably a story teller. If that's the case, you're on a good path to sinking your interview. If you want to fail at ruining your interview, be concise and get to the point quickly.

BE EXCESSIVELY BRIEF / DON'T SELL YOUR STRENGTHS

In the *Preparing for Your Perfect Interview* chapter, I shared an example of a friend of mine who sank interview after interview because he provided one-word answers to questions, and didn't take the opportunity to downplay his weaknesses by sharing his strengths. Let me share a portion of that story from that earlier chapter:

> One day after he learned he hadn't gotten yet another job, I proposed we do a mock interview. In preparation for the interview, I asked him to write down all the questions he could remember from his most recent interview as well as any others he could remember from previous interviews.
>
> He came by my house with a fair number of questions. I told him to answer the questions as he did in the interviews, to the best of his recollection, and I started asking him the questions. The second question I asked him was:
>
> *"Have you ever used XYZ software?"*
>
> *"No."*
>
> *"That's it? You didn't say anything else?"*
>
> *"No."*
>
> I thought I had found a clue as to why he wasn't getting any of the jobs for which he'd interviewed, so I pursued that question a little further. I asked him if he was familiar with the XYZ software, and he said yes, of course, that it was one of the more common software packages in his line of work, but that he'd never used it before. I asked if there were similar software packages that did the same thing and if he had used them. He assured me that was the case – they were critical to the achievement of the work he did. I suggested that a better answer to the XYZ software question may have been:
>
> *"No, I've not used XYZ software before, but I have used ABC and DEF software packages, which do the same thing. I am very adept at software, and there's no question in my mind that I could come up to speed on XYZ software very rapidly."*

So if you want to scuttle your interview, do as my friend was doing – answer briefly, don't explain strengths you have that far out-shine your weaknesses, or at least neutralize them. It's an excellent tactic for losing out in an interview (ask my friend; he did it repeatedly through the years!).

BE A KNOW-IT-ALL

One of my favorite tactics to sink an interview is to be a know-it-all, especially if you are new in a field or profession. So this is an exceptionally important tactic if you are a new graduate.

Many years ago as I was beginning my career, I got a great job in marketing. It so happened that the large company for which I was working was the same company as an older neighbor of mine, who had worked there for several decades. One day he and I were talking and I thought I would impress him with what I knew about the company and our product line. He listened politely and just nodded and smiles as I bragged away. Sigh…it wasn't all that long before I realized that what I had been saying was so naïve – I knew virtually nothing about the company other than a few phrases. What I had been saying was just plain silly…while I was trying to impress him with my great knowledge!

It's a fine line to walk – you don't want to appear stupid, of course, and it's okay to share what you do know. But understand, in the situation you are in, we're not expecting you to know as much as someone who has been doing the job for years. We're looking for foundational skills and knowledge – a foundation we can build on.

But if you want to crush your chances in the interview, be arrogant and come across as someone we won't be able to teach a thing (since you already know everything!).

DON'T TREAT TELEPHONE INTERVIEWS LIKE REAL INTERVIEWS

Earlier in the book I shared the episode about the candidate who obviously has this tactic down well. When you have telephone interviews, to be sure and dash all hopes of getting another interview, take them lightly. Don't prepare. Take the call when you are someplace difficult to have a good, well-thought-out interview. Consider taking the call in a public restroom (the busier the better), while you're driving (if you don't have a convertible, make sure all your windows

Don't be a Know-It-All!

are down), or perhaps at the local grocery store (be sure and finish your shopping during the interview so you will be checking out during the interview).

DO SOMETHING REALLY STUPID AND PUT IT ON FACEBOOK

When it comes to Facebook and job interviews, it's always really impressive to hiring managers to see pictures of you drunk, or defacing public property, or any number of other stupid-human tricks. According to numerous surveys, approximately 80% of employers have looked up potential candidates on Facebook, and 60% of them report having rejected candidates based on what they saw on that social media giant. So if you want to kill any chances you may have of getting a job, be sure and post your most outrageous stunts and actions very publically.

These examples of how to effectively ruin an interview will help you prepare for that upcoming interview. If on the other hand, you want to shine in your interview and really nail it, be sure you do not do any of the things listed in this chapter!

How to Ruin an Interview checklist

_____ Lie

_____ Stalk the hiring manager.

_____ Don't answer questions succinctly. Be vague and mysterious.

_____ Chew gum during my interview.

_____ Make assignments to the hiring manager / recruiter.

_____ Be a story teller – really impress them with my verbal capabilities.

_____ Answer questions with the fewest possible words. Don't sell myself or my strengths.

_____ Be a know-it-all.

_____ Blow off telephone interviews. If they really wanted to consider me as a candidate, they would fly me in.

_____ Put all the stupid things I have done on Facebook – the more the better.

_____ If I follow all these steps, make sure I sign up for unemployment…I will need it for a long time!

Considerations for Recent College Grads

Age is an issue of mind over matter. If you don't mind, it doesn't matter.
– Mark Twain

The New Economy has hit everyone hard, but among the hardest hit are those who have recently graduated or will be graduating soon. I have the opportunity to work every now and then with new graduates to help them get employed, and I thought I would share some of my thoughts about that.

First let me point out the fact that the stereotypical recent college graduate is a twenty-something young man or woman. While that certainly describes many of today's college graduates, there are also many students graduating from college today that are much older than that. Many are in the process of making mid-career changes, and they are facing the same issues as their younger counterparts. So –if you happen to be in the younger segment of the college-graduate population, read on. And – if you happen to be in the more mature segment of the college-graduate population, read on.

First and foremost, don't try to blow the interviewers away with all your knowledge during your interview. As much as you think you know about their business, you simply don't know as much as they know. And that's okay – they would not consider hiring a new graduate if what they were looking for was someone who had the experience someone with five or ten years experience has. They understand and have accepted that you will have a learning curve as you come into their business.

For a decade, I worked at a 250-attorney law firm as their Director of Human Resources. We hired 40% of the attorneys at our firm from the Top Ten law schools in the nation – Yale, Harvard, Stanford, Columbia, University of Virginia, etc. Those students we hired that weren't from the Top 10 law schools needed to be from the Top 50 law schools and had to have graduated in the top 10% of their class. The law students who graduated from these schools were truly intelligent, brilliant people. And yet, conventional wisdom was that for the first two to three years of their careers, their legal secretaries generally knew more about the practice of law than these shining stars from the top schools in the nation!

I have found that to be the case in other industries as well. So when you get an interview with a company, don't try to wow them with what you know. Be confident in what you know, share it if asked, but don't try to come across as a know-it-all, because in most cases you'll just look silly.

As you've read throughout this book, some of the best arrows in your job search quiver will be individuals who you know in the business world. They can assist you in getting your foot in corporate doors, and can make introductions that may lead to career opportunities for you.

While I was writing this book (in fact, less than a week before I wrote this chapter), a vendor who I worked with extensively sent me the following e-mail (the names have been changed):

> Dan,
>
> I would like to introduce you to Andrew Johnson. Andrew is a *recent graduate* of the University of Northern Colorado, Greeley with a *BA degree in Environmental and Sustainability Studies*. Andrew is targeting opportunities where he can apply his degree as well as his *critical thinking* and *problem-solving skills*. Andrew has a *particular passion around municipal water*. I can personally speak to Andrew's *outstanding character* and am *happy to recommend him* for any position you may have at the City for which he is qualified. Attached please find a copy of Andrew's resume.

Tyler, Dan Quillen is the Director of Internal Services at the City of Aurora. He is one of the top HR talents in town and I am proud to call him both a client and a friend. I recommend you get to know Dan as you embark on your career path which I know will have many great adventures in the years ahead.

Dan, meet Tyler … Tyler meet Dan.

Best regards to you both!

Terry

What's not to like about that introduction?! When I received that e-mail, it did not have italics – I added them to highlight the things I learned about this young man, a potential candidate for a position at the city where I work. Here are those things:

Andrew:

- is a recent graduate;

- has a BA degree in Environmental and Sustainability Studies;

- has critical thinking and problem-solving skills;

- has a particular passion around municipal water;

- has an outstanding character.

- And the fellow who I know and trust is happy to recommend him.

I have hired many employees through the years – hundreds at least, perhaps a thousand. As good as I am at reviewing resumes, interviewing and selecting candidates, every now and then I am fooled and hire a real clunker. Sometimes it is scary hiring someone from a one- or two-page resume and one or two 45-minute interviews. Whenever I can get an endorsement like the one above from someone whose judgment I trust, that candidate generally goes to the top of my list, and the job is his / hers to lose in the interview process.

What does that mean for you? It means you should seek out individuals who can endorse you. At this stage of your career you probably won't have a lot of former bosses or co-workers that can provide support like this, so it may be a long-time family friend (which was the case in the example above), a next-door neighbor, etc.

Who could introduce me and strongly recommend me for a job?

When you finally get your interview, don't try to guess what the hiring manager is looking for...be yourself. In an earlier chapter I talked about the interview being a sales call, where you are the sales person, and the product you are selling is yourself. What happens if you sell them on something you are not and they hire you? In that scenario, it will likely not end well for you. So just be yourself.

When I was seeking a job during the recession, a savvy professional whom I know was helping me with my job hunt, and he observed that I might be experiencing age discrimination during some of my job interviews. I had earned many interviews, had the skills, experience and education to fill all those jobs, but just wasn't getting any job offers. He suggested that I craft a short spiel I could give at the end of my interviews, to counter the stereotype many people have of older workers (I was 55 years old at the time, and thanks to male pattern baldness, looked even older than that!) Here are the stereotypical things some people (especially younger hiring managers) think about older workers:

- they don't have much more time to work – if I hire this guy, he'll be here for a year or two and then retire;

- they can't learn new software;

- they don't get along with younger workers;

- they are always sick.

I prepared remarks I could share at the end of an interview when the hiring manager asked if I had any questions or would like to share anything about myself we hadn't already discussed. Here's what I said when asked if I had anything I would like to share:

> Yes, I do. But first, I'd like to share some information with you that you can't ask me. But since I am sharing it freely, there is no problem. I don't want to make you feel uncomfortable, but I would like to address a couple of topics.
>
> **(By now, I had their attention!)**
>
> As you may have noticed, I am probably older than most of the other applicants. But I want you to know that I have a lot of runway left on my career – I am not considering retirement any time soon. I have three children who are in college for a number more years, and besides, I am nowhere near being ready to retire.
>
> **(That dispels their concern that I will retire as soon as I get trained.)**
>
> I am very good at learning new software. I have been at this so long that I have used many different software packages, and have never had difficulties picking up new applications or software packages.
>
> **(That addresses any concerns they have about whether or not I can learn new software or work with new technology.)**
>
> I enjoy all ages of workers and work well with younger workers as well as workers my age.
>
> **(So much for the concerns about me being a crabby old man…)**
>
> And I am very healthy. I have worked 50 hours a week for most of my career, and have no reason to expect I will work less in this position.
>
> **(And now they know I am healthy and they don't have to worry about me being sick all the time.)**
>
> In addition, the benefit to you is that you get an HR professional with years of HR experience. I have been doing HR so long, there are very few things that surprise me – I have seen it all. Because of that, I don't get too excited or agitated about anything that comes up.

(Adding a cherry on top – not only do they not have to worry about me as an older worker, but they actually benefit from it!)

For the purposes of this book, I wish I could tell you I used this approach many times. But I didn't – I used it only once. But…I am batting 1000 when using it – I got every job for which I applied when I used that dialogue!

And this may surprise you, but young people face age discrimination as well. Only the age discrimination they face isn't illegal, as it is for people over 40 years of age.

What are the stereotypes that might plague young job-search candidates? Here are a few stereotypes of young workers (especially from Baby Boomers):

- they have a poor work ethic;

- they have an entitlement mentality;

- they job hop;

- they are egocentric;

- they dress too casually for the workplace.

Ouch! If I were a younger worker trying to break into a career job, I might prepare a short spiel similar to what I prepared and delivered as an older worker. So when the 50-something hiring manager asks you if there's anything you'd like to add at the end of your interview, you can say:

Yes, I do. I appreciate the opportunity to interview with you, and I'd like to take a moment to share a few things about myself that may surprise you.

As you may have noticed, I may be one of your younger applicants. I know some of my peers have a poor reputation because of their work ethic, but I learned to work hard from an early age. When I was twelve years old, my older brother and I shared a paper route. Every morning we rolled out of bed at 4:00am and bagged the newspapers so we could deliver them before dawn. He drove, and I pitched the newspapers. I kept that job from age twelve until I headed off to college.

(That dispels their concern that you have a poor work ethic.)

My parents were excellent teachers, and one of the lessons I learned well at their hands was that I needed to earn whatever I received – no one was waiting at the door to reward me for merely showing up – I had to work for whatever I got.

(That addresses any concerns about you having an entitlement mentality.)

I have had two jobs since I was twelve years old – the newspaper route I mentioned earlier and I cooked breakfast at the student center all four years I was in college.

(So much for the concerns about you being a job hopper.)

When I was in high school and college, I was an athlete and played on many teams. I learned quickly that it wasn't all about me – it was about the team. I supported my team mates and they supported me. I knew I had to work hard so that the team could succeed.

(And now they know you have the ability to sacrifice for others to the betterment of the team – it's not all about you.)

Some of my peers tend to dress very casually. That's not me. As you can see today, I understand that I am applying for a job in the business world – not as a landscape gardener or GAP clothing store salesperson.

(Now they know you will dress appropriately at work.)

Meet age
discrimination
head-on.

These have been just a few thoughts I wanted to share about young – and older – candidates as you enter – or re-enter – the work force.

Considerations for Recent College Graduates checklist

_____ Remember – employers will hire me even if I don't know everything!

_____ Find someone who knows me well enough to introduce me to hiring managers with positive, glowing comments.

_____ Be myself in the interview – don't try to be something I am not.

_____ Don't try to guess what the hiring manager is looking for.

_____ Deal with age discrimination head on – don't let stereotypes linger.

Stay Positive!

Worry often gives a small thing a big shadow.
— Swedish Proverb

One of the things I have noticed in working with individuals who have been out of work for a period of time (very typical in this economy) is that they are often plagued with depression, anxiety and worry.

I think that's natural. I am by nature a pretty optimistic person. Put me in a room filled with manure, and I will be positive there must be a pony in there somewhere! Notwithstanding that cheery outlook on life, I have to admit that when I was laid off in 2011, I became aware of occasional doubts and worries creeping in. But I was able to fend those negative thoughts off, and we'll talk about ways you can do that.

But first — it's important that you pay attention to those kinds of feelings within yourself. They can be devastating to your job search. Depression can seep through from your subconscious into cover letters, interviews, even your resumes. It can cause you to think, "What's the difference?" on the very day the perfect job for you is posted…the one that will end your unemployment…and you don't apply for it, because you've taken time off your job search for a couple days…which turns into a week…which becomes several months. At the end of that period, you're still out of work, and more disillusioned than ever.

Sound familiar? If so – do something about it. You cannot reclaim those days, weeks and months or the jobs that could have been. But you can buckle down and jump back in the job search game.

So – what can you do to stay positive? In *Get a Job!*, I spend quite a bit of time discussing that topic. For example, following are ten keys I offered for my readers' consideration as they strive to remain positive:

- Keep busy.

- Start an exercise program.

- Change your mindset.

- Marshall your resources.

- Remember – 20,000,000+ Americans.

- Don't be a victim.

- Set a schedule.

- Get plenty of sleep.

- Prepare for the long haul.

- Build in some entertainment.

- Hang in there!

Let me address each of these keys briefly. (For a more complete treatment of this topic, you may wish to pick up *Get a Job!*) And yes, I know I said there were ten keys, and I have listed eleven keys. I always like to deliver more than I have promised.

Key # 1. Keep busy. All of these points are important, but this may be one of the main points. Keep yourself busy, but make sure your busyness is job related. It is so easy to make yourself busy in activities that do not move your job search forward. Insist on working 40 hours a week on finding a job…this includes searching for job openings, submitting applications, reaching out to your network, preparing for interviews, doing mock interviews, etc.

Key # 2. Start an exercise program. Studies have shown that one of the best ways to beat depression is to have an effective exercise program. Of course you should check with your doctor first – he or she can prescribe a physical exercise regimen that will help you stay in shape and battle depressing thoughts that may creep in.

Key # 3. Change your mindset. I am referring here to your *financial* mindset. You have moved into a chapter of your life where you must be especially mindful of the monies you spend. Instead of buying books on Amazon.com or your favorite local bookseller, start haunting your local library. Many times, books will be available there to assist with your job hunt – the very books you might spend several hundred dollars purchasing.

You must have Internet access to be effective in your job search. But – I am well aware that Internet service can be very expensive. If that becomes an expense you have to shed, then again, head over to the local library where you'll find Internet access aplenty.

Key # 4. Marshal your resources. You should immediately take stock of your financial needs, and what monies you have to meet those needs. Can you access your 401(k) (even if you have to pay some penalties)? Can you sell anything of value to help make ends meet? I have a friend who lost his job one year in May, and he immediately sold his ski boat. He figured if he waited until the end of the water skiing season, he might be unable to sell the boat, or if he was able to sell it, he'd have to take less money for it. He traded in his wife's BMW for a car that was still functional but much less expensive. He economized. In a pinch, can family members pitch in to assist you?

Key # 5. Remember – 20,000,000+ Americans. Remember you're in good company when it comes to those who are unemployed in this country. While that won't put food on the table and pay the mortgage or electric bill, don't lose sight of the fact that many other Americans are out of work through no fault of their own. We discussed in the opening chapters of this book what a fable the government-reported unemployment rate is, so don't let that get you down.

Key # 6. Don't be a victim. I have worked with many job seekers through the years, and invariably those who take the longest to find work are those who spend time blaming others for their unemployment situation. Leave it be – look forward and not backward. Put all your energies into getting that Perfect Interview so you can snag that Perfect Job!

Key # 7. Set a schedule. We talked about the importance of setting a schedule in the *How to Get That Interview* chapter earlier in the book. If you neglect this step, I guarantee you will have time leaks in your day and week that will negatively impact your job search. Craft a schedule and stick to it, especially when / if you're feeling down. A schedule will help you pull through and help you be successful in your job search.

Key # 8. Get plenty of sleep. Your mother always preached the need for you to get plenty of sleep, and she was right. I know how easy it is to stay up late into the night and sleep in during the day, and it's not conducive to a fruitful job hunt. Adequate amounts of sleep will help you remain healthy and help your attitude. Studies indicate one of the best ways to fight depression and anxiety is to get sufficient sleep. So – make sure you get sufficient sleep!

Key # 9. Prepare for the long haul. Prepare yourself mentally (and financially) to be out of work for a long time. I've shared with you my experience with networking groups and how long some of those folks had been out of work. I don't say this (Prepare for the long haul) to frighten or discourage you. Let this mindset work within you to encourage you to be active and aggressive in your job search – there's no time to let any grass grow under your job-searching feet!

STAY POSITIVE!

Key # 10. Build in some entertainment. Be aware of the need to have entertainment in your life – and the lives of those closest to you. Remembering Key # 3 (Change your mindset), this probably doesn't mean you'll drop $30 for a tub of popcorn and an evening at the movies with your sweetheart – maybe instead it's a $1 movie from Redbox and some microwave popcorn. But treat yourself every once in awhile. Perhaps a drive along the ocean, or through your favorite nearby grove of trees, or that winding dirt road up in the mountains will help soothe your soul. Whatever it takes, don't shut down this important aspect of your life.

Key # 11. Hang in there! Finally – hang in there! This time in your life will be over sooner than you think. Hopefully in the future as you look back on this experience, you can do so with introspection and insight, perhaps even fondness. It is easy to be professional when everything is going your way. But real professionalism manifests itself during adversity.

Stay Positive! checklist

_____ Maintain a positive attitude…if I don't, it may come through in my cover letters, interviews, etc.

_____ I must guard against depression, worry and anxiety – all are natural, but I cannot give in to them for even one day.

_____ I should set a schedule that will help me stay busy and keep me focused on the job at hand – finding a job!

_____ I can do this. This time in my life will be over soon, and I will be employed once again.

_____ Believe that last bullet point, and work to make it happen.

Stay busy. Exercise. Sleep. Rent a movie!

Index

THE PERFECT INTERVIEW

NOTES

NOTES

THE PERFECT INTERVIEW

NOTES

NOTES

THE PERFECT INTERVIEW

NOTES